Scandi Modern

Calm, Cosy Living

Rebecca Lawson & Reena Simon

Photography by Benjamin Edwards

MITCHELL BEAZLEY

Contents

INTRODUCTION

We first met in 2016 – two mothers connecting over Instagram DMs, kitchen-table chats and a shared love of interiors and Scandinavia. What began as a friendship soon grew; we started hosting face-to-face events for our online communities, celebrating all things home, and eventually published our first book together, *Scandi Rustic*.

When we wrote that book, the world had suddenly slowed. The global Covid-19 pandemic and lockdown meant that we were all inside more than ever, craving warmth and comfort, and our homes became our safe places. That book was a love letter to cosiness – to the textures, palettes and interior design touches that helped us feel cocooned through each day.

Nearly ten years on, we're still close friends as well as creative partners. Our children are older now, our days busier and our homes are asked to do more.

We now have kitchens and bedrooms that spend their days doubling as offices; living rooms host movie nights as well as workout sessions. The pace of life has returned and, with it, new possibilities for how our homes can support us.

We've both moved and renovated: one of us a 1930s home, the other a 1960s bungalow. Both were blank canvases, now completely transformed. Unlike the period houses we'd known before, these homes have modern bones: bigger windows, open layouts, cleaner lines. They asked different questions of us.

How do you keep warmth in a space built for light? How do you make modern architecture feel cocooning as well as contemporary? How do you bring character to homes without ornate details to fall back on?

That's where *Scandi Modern* began. It is more than an aesthetic, it's a lifestyle. It invites us to slow down, design with care and create spaces that feel truly lived-in.

A Scandi Modern home is a space that evolves with you – that feels effortless. Every piece has been chosen with care, not accumulated by impulse. It's walking into a room and sensing that it just works, not because it follows trends, but because it has been shaped by life, memory and intention.

In this book, we look at the ways our new homes, as well as the ones we have visited, have been shaped into places that feel calm but not cold. These homes are practical but never stark.

Scandi Modern is our way of sharing what we've learned about the foundations of this design approach and the styling details that make it feel effortless. More than anything, we hope to show you how to style your own spaces with confidence – to create rooms that don't just look beautiful in photographs, but feel good to live in every day. Homes for busy mornings and quiet evenings. Homes which, above all, feel like the place you most want to be.

FOUNDATIONS OF STYLE

Foundations of Style

Every home begins with choices. Some are big: where to position the kitchen island, what floor to lay. Others are small: which mug you reach for in the morning, where to curate a cosy corner to catch the morning sun. There aren't hard-and-fast rules. There are only ways of seeing – lenses you can hold up to any space. These guide us when we're deciding what to bring in, what to leave out, and how to create homes that feel not only beautiful but also lived in. You can already sense the atmosphere: pale timber, natural textures and soft daylight falling across simple vignettes. The calm here comes not from abundance but from restraint, each element having been chosen with care. The six foundations of Scandi Modern are:

1
FUNCTION MEETS FEELING

2
CURATION OVER DECORATION

3
MATERIALS THAT LAST

4
LIGHTING AS A DESIGN TOOL

5
LET NATURE BE YOUR GUIDE

6
RITUALS

Each of these foundations will unfold over the pages that follow, not as fixed instructions, but as guiding threads, showing how atmosphere is built, piece by piece, and how the Scandi Modern approach can be adapted for any home.

1

Function Meets Feeling

Scandinavian style is sometimes misread as purely utilitarian. But functionality is only half the story; atmosphere, materiality and ritual are what give this aesthetic its enduring appeal. And the story of 'function meets feeling' lies in the details that underpin practical choices: the depth of a sofa, the placement of a table, the presence of a peg rail in the hall. These decisions define not only how a room works, but how it feels.

When Reena renovated her kitchen, she set the oak dining table by the floor-to-ceiling windows. It was a practical decision concerning layout and space. But the effect was powerful: the table became a natural gathering point, lit by the morning sun. Even on grey days, daylight and the view of trees framed by the window turns everyday meals into calm rituals.

In a Danish ground-floor apartment we visited, a handmade oak island was designed as a work surface, yet its placement transformed the flow of the home. It became the heart of daily life – a spot for passing plates, leaning in to chat and sharing moments together.

One of the key elements of this foundation is that arrangement matters. Even the simplest pieces – a sofa, a table, a row of hooks – when chosen and placed with care, shape how a room feels as well as how it functions.

2

Curation over Decoration

Every home needs decoration, but it's easy to overfill shelves so that they are stacked with ornaments, crowd walls with frames and clutter surfaces – all for the sake of adding. Scandi Modern shifts the focus. It's less about decoration, more about curation: choosing fewer things with greater care.

What strikes you most about the homes in this book isn't what's there, but what's left out. A single ceramic vase sits alone on a worktop. A painting is hung low, given space to breathe. A dining table dressed only with linen is lit by the flicker of candlelight.

When there is less, what remains matters more. A handmade bowl picked up while travelling; a stack of books read and reread; a photograph that anchors a space in memory – these objects carry weight not because they are many, but because they are chosen.

When we moved into our new homes, we tended to crowded mantelpieces with trinkets and frames. One day, Reena stripped back her display to just three things: a family photo, a candle and a small ceramic vessel. The room felt lighter. The glow of the candle became more present.

This is the essence of the foundation: curation brings clarity. By choosing carefully and leaving space around the things you love, you allow them – and your home – to breathe.

Materials that Last

At the heart of Scandi Modern are materials chosen for
honesty and endurance. Wood, stone, linen and wool stand up
to daily life and grow more beautiful with time.

Timber darkens with age, linen creases, stone carries the marks of each season. These are not flaws, but stories, and reminders that homes are for living in, not preserving. A solid oak table, a linen sofa, a stone basin – each one becomes more characterful as it wears in, not out.

By contrast, synthetic surfaces that pretend to be something else often disappoint. They may look flawless at first, but they don't wear well.

We chose microcement and polished concrete floors for our kitchens. They once worried us: every scratch and crack seemed like a problem. Now, after years of living with these surfaces, the traces and marks have a life of their own. These floors have history and character.

In the bathroom pictured here, the carved stone basin is another example of furniture with a story to tell. Its cool, rough-hewn texture is so tactile it becomes the focal point of the room. Little else is needed – the material itself tells the story. Just as with a timber island or a well-worn table, the beauty lies in the substance and not the adornment.

Materials that last grow with us. They carry memory in every mark, reminding us that beauty lies not in perfection, but in endurance.

4

Lighting as a Design Tool

In Scandinavia, as elsewhere in the North, winters can be long
and dark. To counter this, we lean into lighting. It isn't just practical;
it sets the mood, marks the hours and carries the day.

Lighting is emotional as much as functional. The Danish concept of *hygge* is often linked to cosiness, but it is inseparable from light: candlelight, firelight, lamplight. Atmosphere is crafted deliberately.

That's why, in Scandi Modern, light is treated as a design tool. It is considered as carefully as furniture or materials, because the way a room is lit determines how it feels. Daylight is maximized through sheer window dressings, pale walls and open layouts. Mirrors bounce brightness into corners. At night, artificial light is layered – pools, lamps, pendants, candles – rather than glaring from a single source.

Our living rooms never rely on one single ceiling pendant. The effect would be flat, almost clinical. Adding a floor lamp in one corner and a table lamp by the sofa transforms the space instantly, creating a calm and inviting mood.

And then there is the light we love the most: dappled light – that fleeting, shifting glow falling across floors and walls. We really enjoyed watching it in so many of the homes we visited on our travels; it was a reminder of the season itself. At certain hours of the day, it drifts across walls and floors, altering the atmosphere, and instantly enlivens rooms.

5

Let Nature be your Guide

In Scandi Modern, nature is not an afterthought, it is a guiding principle. Homes are designed in conversation with the natural world, which guides choices in colour, texture and flow.

This relationship with nature shows most clearly in palettes and materials. Colours are drawn from the outdoors: muted greens, soft greys, sandy neutrals. Materials echo the earth: timber, stone, clay, linen. A sprig of blossom in spring; herbs gathered in summer; pine in winter – each gesture ties a home to the seasons.

Ignore nature and a space often feels unsettled: heavy curtains block out light, synthetic tones jar with the view outside. Invite nature in and a home begins to breathe. At Jon and Sofia's family home in Sweden (pages 152–65), large timber-framed windows look out onto a lush treescape, and the palette inside – chalky white walls, pale oak, soft wool throws – echoes the view. The boundary between inside and out is blurred; the landscape is made part of the home's design.

Sometimes it is even simpler: a handful of branches, a vase of wildflowers or, as in Reena's bathroom, dried florals lining a windowsill, can bring the season indoors. When the outdoors shapes what's inside, homes feel calmer, more grounded and connected to the world beyond their walls.

6

Rituals

The final foundation that brings everything together: rituals.
Function, curation, materials, lighting and nature set the scene,
but it is the rituals they support that make a house feel lived in.

In Scandinavia, our homeowners shared how they shape their routines into something more: meals by candlelight, weekend baking, blankets pulled close by the fire. Their homes have been styled to make space for these moments.

A throw on a sofa or a stack of books by the bed, the trace of wax from last night's candle on the table – these objects serve the lives unfolding around them.

Every Friday in Rebecca's kitchen, she lights candles before sitting down to pizza as a family. This is the only night of the week with no after-school activities, so everyone can finally slow down. The smell of melted cheese, the sound of cutlery, the glow of candlelight – together the family mark the end of the week.

At the two Mallorcan homes we visited (pages 118–35, 136–51), meals were often cooked outdoors, with a barbecue lit in the garden and lanterns strung across the terrace. Eating outside was more than convenience, it was a ritual of connection, in which gathering gives a home its spirit.

For both of us, preparing tablescapes for special occasions shows how even the simple act of laying the table can become a ritual.

In Scandi Modern, rituals are easy, repeatable acts that make daily life feel intentional as well as beautiful.

ROOM BY ROOM

Room by Room

The foundations of Scandi Modern are not rules. They are lenses through which to see a home, and they remind us that every choice matters. The aim is not perfection, but intention.

Together, these foundations create homes that are styled with balance, considering aesthetic alongside practicality, restraint with warmth, and timelessness as it interacts with the demands of daily life.

If we look again at these foundations, we will notice not just how these spaces look, but how they feel: calm, tactile, connected. Dappled light across a table. Views out to nature. Materials that invite touch. A table laid with care, ready for a shared meal. Close your eyes and you can almost smell the coffee or hear the crackle of the fire. That is Scandi Modern. Now we will explore with you, room by room, how to style your home.

The Living Room

For us, growing up in the 1980s and 1990s, family leisure time meant Saturday night television: sofas lined up to face the screen, snacks on the coffee table, everyone gathering to watch the same show. The whole family paused together, laughter and conversation spilling out between programmes. The living room was where we came together almost without thinking, the unquestioned heart of the home.

Today, life looks different. Screens travel with us, and our families do not always gather around a single focal point in quite the same way. Yet the living room still matters. It is still the place to which we retreat at the end of the day, the place where conversations start. The question is not whether we still need a living room, but how to make it feel calming and purposeful again. The answer lies in the Scandi Modern style foundations and finding new rituals for life as we live it today.

In Reena's own home, the Stuv woodburning stove provides a focal point. Shelving in the same finish as the walls keeps the colour palette consistent and calm. An oversized wool rug grounds the space, and the low-level light keeps the room low-key and welcoming. These design details have created a tactile, inviting space towards which people naturally gravitate.

In Sweden, at the home of Jon and Sofia (pages 152–65), two chairs in leather and sheepskin face inward, showing how a living room can be arranged for conversation rather than for a television. In Mallorca (pages 118–35), Namali's living room is centred on two oak coffee tables, intentionally placed side by side and with art and design books stacked together, inviting people to pause and read. The oak surfaces, textured almost like bark, soften and complement the backdrop of tall steel windows. The double-height space feels *hygge* despite its size.

What ties all these spaces together is the way light is used. Glowing floor lamps and candles soften corners, making these modern living rooms feel cocooning after dark.

The lesson is simple: the arrangement of cosy seating invites you in, but comfort holds you there. A fireplace that becomes a gathering point, a chair placed with intention, a coffee table that softens the space, a lamp that warms it by night – these are the choices that make a living room feel alive. Calm, tactile and connected: the essence of Scandi Modern.

Create Conversation

Angle two statement chairs towards each other to encourage dialogue and connection, as Jon and Sofia (pages 152–65) have done in their open-plan living space. Here the vintage Swedese Laminett easy chair captures the balance between craftsmanship and comfort, its gentle curves and sheepskin seat inviting you to linger. Keep the centre of the room open to encourage flow, using a low table to ground the space. Underfoot, a richly textured rug from Ferm Living or The White Company adds texture and warmth, softening the acoustics. Let daylight move across the surfaces and light a candle as evening draws in.

Let Seating Breathe

Pull seating slightly away from walls so it stands confidently within the room. This small shift can transform the feeling of a space, creating flow and a sense of ease. In Oliver and Michelle's calm living area (pages 198–215), a linen sofa and GUBI's Pacha lounge chair show how freestanding pieces can feel both relaxed and refined. The GUBI Gravity table lamp softens a corner, casting gentle light and shadow. Space, light and form shape mood as powerfully as colour, and when furniture sits forward, the room feels open, balanced and effortlessly intentional.

Balance in Clusters

Style a coffee table with purpose and restraint. Group objects in odd numbers: three or five pieces tends to feel most natural and balanced. Mix materials and forms: a Georg Jensen candleholder, a stack of books and a hand-thrown ceramic bowl each bring their own shape, texture and tone. Play with height and proportion, raising smaller items on books and offsetting taller vases with lower, grounding pieces. Use one table, such as GUBI's Epic, or layer two to add dimension and flow. Once arranged, step back and remove one thing – a little editing keeps the composition calm, cohesive and effortless.

Light in Layers

Treat lighting as you would furniture: each piece defines how a room feels. In a living space, include pendant and floor lighting to create depth and direct light where it's needed most. A sculptural focal point such as the Audo Copenhagen Dancing pendant by Iskos-Berlin (top right) brings softness from above, while the Artek A810 floor lamp by Alvar Aalto (top left) adds a mid-century note of timeless form. The oversized GUBI floor lamp in Helena and Jakob's living room (pages 166–83 and opposite) grounds the room with quiet strength and proportion. Fit all lighting on dimmers so you can direct light throughout the day – bright and functional by morning, warm and atmospheric by night.

The Dining Room

In the past, a dining room was one of the most formal rooms in the house – a separate space, when broken-plan living was the norm. When we were young, we remember the dining room being saved for Sunday roasts or Christmas dinners, with heavy tables, matching chairs and china stored in sideboards, rarely seeing the light of day. The rest of the week, that room sat in waiting, more about show than daily life.

Scandi Modern homes tell a different story. Few have separate dining rooms and, in Scandinavia in particular, gathering around a table is a more relaxed affair. More often, the table sits in an open-plan living space and it never feels like an afterthought. The table is home to everyday rituals; it is somewhere for children to do homework, where laptops open at lunchtime and suppers with friends stretch into the evening.

In Rebecca's home (pages 88–105), an oval dining table from Another Country, laid with linen, candles and foraged greenery, shows how atmosphere matters more than occasion. Rebecca intentionally chose an oval shape to soften the sharp angles of the kitchen extension.

At Kine and Kristoffer's house in Mallorca (pages 136–51), the couple built their dining table themselves from bamboo (a material chosen for its sustainability), their craftsmanship giving the piece a warmth that no factory-made furniture could hope to replicate.

And on the Swedish coast, at Jon and Sofia's home (pages 152–65), a table positioned by wide windows frames the sea beyond, proving that dining can be about connection to the landscape as much as to other people.

These spaces remind us that the dining table is no longer about rare occasions: it's about daily connection. A well-chosen surface, chairs that invite you to linger, and the glow of candlelight or morning sun: these are the details that make a dining table an integral part of family life.

Design for Different Dining

An extendable dining table offers flexibility – compact for everyday use, generous when guests arrive. In Jon and Sofia's Swedish coastal home (pages 152–65), the Mi 901 table by Bruno Mathsson sits with classic wooden chairs by &Tradition, which mirror its light, functional form. Above, a Flos Smithfield pendant light defines the centre of the room, while an iconic Stoff Nagel candleholder by Stoff Copenhagen adds height and structure to the table surface. Keep day-to-day styling minimal to maintain space for movement. When entertaining, extend the table and layer simple candlelight or greenery to shift the mood from 'everyday' to 'occasion'.

Circular Suits Small Spaces

Choose a circular dining table to soften angular rooms and improve flow, especially where space is tight. The absence of corners makes movement easier and encourages conversation to circulate naturally. In their narrow dining area, Kine and Kristoffer (pages 136–51) designed and built their own table from lightweight, sustainable bamboo, showing how hands-on craftsmanship can bring both warmth and practicality. Pair with simple stools or benches to keep the lines open and the feeling calm.

TABLESCAPING

Tablescaping (noun): the art of arranging a dining table in a decorative way, often with linens, flowers, candles and objects that enhance the experience of a meal.

While the word 'tablescaping' can sound formal, in Scandi Modern homes it's never about perfection. Instead, it's about creating atmosphere. A thoughtfully set table signals more than an opportunity to eat – it marks a moment.

During the week, tables often house the clutter of everyday life: laptops, schoolwork, plates set down between comings and goings. But something changes at the weekend, or when friends arrive. A linen cloth pulled from the cupboard, a jug of wild branches, a row of candles down the centre – small gestures like these shift the mood. Suddenly, even family pizza night feels like an occasion.

In Mallorca (pages 118–35), Namali dresses her table with simple earthenware plates and tumblers in sea-glass tones – proof that everyday pieces can feel special when chosen with care. In Gothenburg (pages 166–83), Helena and Jakob choose plants from their garden to serve as a centrepiece, echoing the surrounding landscape.

Tablescaping in Scandi Modern homes is never about layers of excess. Just one or two thoughtful details are enough to remind us that the table is not only where we dine, but where we gather and reconnect.

Make the Everyday Feel Special

Sometimes a beautiful, material-led dining table does the hard work for you. The Epic table by GUBI, with its sculptural travertine base, sets the tone before anything is placed on top. Layer simple, functional pieces: Ferm Living glassware, Audo Copenhagen candleholders and hand-thrown ceramics that vary in tone and glaze. Add a decorative butter knife or small utensil to show care in the everyday. Overhead, the Vitra Akari 21A pendant light by Isamu Noguchi diffuses a warm light that pools over the table surface, creating focus without formality. Even when setting a place for one, take a moment to make it feel special – a reminder that good design supports how you live, not just how a space looks. Keep arrangements simple and give each piece room to breathe; the table's natural material and form will do the rest.

Dining under the Sky

Style an outdoor table with the same intention you bring to the indoors – calm, useful and pared back. Start with simple, natural materials: a striped linen tablecloth from Broste Copenhagen or Tine K Home, pale wood furniture and clear glassware that catches the light. Add quiet contrast through cutlery; the Grove set from Scandi Living pairs stainless steel with FSC-certified bamboo, balancing warmth and polish while remaining comfortable in the hand. Keep the palette soft and sun-faded so that it blends easily with the surroundings. Forage from your garden for finishing touches; dried wheat, wild grasses or herbs in a small vase add shape and scent. Choose lightweight pieces that can be moved easily as the light changes. Outdoor dining should feel relaxed but deliberate – an effortless extension of your home.

The Kitchen

The kitchen has always been the hardest-working room in the house –
a place for preparing meals, washing up, keeping the household running.
In broken-plan layouts it can often feel cut off from the rest of the home. In
Scandi Modern homes, however, open-plan layouts prevail, bringing together
living, dining and kitchen spaces, and creating greater connection. In these
homes, the kitchen is the hub. Kitchen designs now frequently include islands,
which act as additional worktop space but also an anchor around which
conversations can start and people gather informally.

At Helena and Jakob's home (pages 166–83) on the Swedish coast, the open-
plan kitchen is designed around light and material. Stone and timber echo
the rocky landscape outside, while generous windows frame views of sea
and sky. The space is practical, yes, but also deeply connected to its setting.

In Reena's own home (pages 70–87), open shelving has become the key
feature. Plates, glasses and ceramics are stacked in view, chosen carefully
so that nothing feels cluttered. Each piece earns its place, and together they
bring warmth and character.

In Denmark, architect Mette converted part of her home (pages 184–97) into
a kitchen design showroom. At its heart is a spacious kitchen island in oak
– designed by Mette with open shelving to showcase ceramic pieces. This
design choice elevates the island beyond functionality, transforming it into
a striking focal point that adds to the atmosphere of the room.

What these kitchens share is intention. Materials are chosen to bring calm,
shelving is styled to celebrate the everyday and islands become stages on
which life can unfold. Scandi Modern kitchens remind us that simplicity
is not about doing less, but about doing only what matters.

Work with Wood

Rebecca's kitchen captures the essence of Scandi Modern design: quiet, functional and grounded in materiality. By juxtaposing open shelves with closed cabinetry she has combined display and discretion. Choose open shelves for texture and everyday pieces, and closed cabinets to create visual calm. Pair oak with polished chrome worktops to create contrast, and so that the palette does not feel flat. Keep tones consistent across floors and shelving, so the wood's grain remains the focus. Style shelves with intention. Group ceramics and glassware loosely and leave space so that the materials can breathe. Introduce one black detail – it could be a fitting, handle or stool leg – to ground the lightness. The result is modern utility shaped by natural warmth.

Balance Warmth and Contrast

If choosing darker cabinetry – like the Sebastian Cox for deVOL kitchen in Reena's home (above) – brighten the space with worktops in pale concrete (such as Caesarstone Topus) to reflect light and open up the room. Create contrast through materiality; the OKA stools Reena chose set woven warmth against the cool, honed stone. Keep styling minimal – one or two pieces per surface – to maintain flow. Introduce soft neutral ceramics or pendant lights in pale tones at eye level to balance darker cabinetry. Fit dimmers so you can shift from task-bright to ambient evening light.

Introduce Depth through Colour

Scandi Modern design isn't limited to pale woods and whites. Darker tones can feel just as calm when balanced with light and texture. Choose deep cabinetry colours such as graphite, navy or forest green to echo nature, then pair with luxe materials like marble or honed stone for contrast. Reflect light through surface choice and style: a waterfall island or splashback in marble catches the natural light and keeps the palette bright. Anchor the look with sculptural lighting: the Audo Copenhagen TR Bulb Suspension Frame pendant shown here defines the narrow space without overpowering it, drawing the eye lengthways and balancing the weight of the island below – proof that, even in smaller spaces, considered materials and proportion bring the design together.

The Bedroom

Of all the rooms in the house, the bedroom is the easiest to neglect – piles of laundry, cluttered side tables – yet it's the space we rely on most to restore us. In the Scandi Modern homes we visited, bedrooms were the most pared back of all, proving that less is more when it comes to rest.

These rooms weren't sparse for the sake of style. They were intentional: fabric-upholstered or timber-framed beds to ground the space, surfaces left clear so texture and light could take the lead. With fewer distractions, the atmosphere felt calm by default.

In Denmark, Oliver (pages 198–215) designed bespoke timber panelling that stretches across the room, its natural grain softening the modern lines of his apartment. In Mallorca, Namali (pages 118–35) created a serene retreat for her daughter, with soft linen bedding, clusters of tactile jute pendant lights either side of the bed and an artwork in soft blush tones above. Rebecca's (pages 88–105) London bedroom was designed to feel like a luxury hotel suite, with a reeded glass room divider creating a gentle partition between dressing room and bedroom. To anchor the sleeping space, Rebecca chose a tactile bouclé fabric bedframe, layering it with cushions. On the Swedish coast, Jon and Sofia's (pages 152–65) simple bedroom, with a low bed and linen curtains moving in the breeze, proves how little is needed to make a room feel whole.

With three girls filling the rest of the house with energy, Reena and her husband sacrificed the tradition of a rarely used spare room to create a suite-like space that connects sleeping and living – more hotel than home. The palette is muted, the surfaces kept clear and the flow between the two rooms offers a quiet sense of retreat – a reminder that purposeful rooms will always serve a family better than spaces kept 'just in case'.

The lesson is clear: bedrooms don't need to be filled, they need to hold space. It is this restraint that makes bedrooms in Scandi Modern homes feel like true retreats.

Layer for Rest, not Clutter

In a Scandi Modern bedroom, calm begins with colour. Work with warm neutrals: stone, sand, oat and clay. These are tones that soften light and feel restful through every season. Layer tactile materials like Tekla linen, wool and bouclé – for their tactility rather than as excess decoration. Choose curved shapes and upholstered linen headboards to balance architectural form and keep surfaces minimal: a marble side table from H&M Home or a small stool is enough. Hang artwork above the bed simply, with space around it. Comfort here is built through proportion, texture and tone.

Light with Intention

In a Scandi Modern bedroom, lighting should define how the room feels and functions and be planned as part of the architecture from the outset. Choose sculptural fittings that add shape without dominating. In Rebecca's guest bedroom (opposite), Spark & Bell globe wall lights bring soft symmetry and a diffused light that flatters the natural materials. Choose a pendant that balances shape and material, like the Michael Anastassiades Ball (top right), where opal glass meets polished metal to create contrast and refinement. Include directional lighting, such as the Vipp 524 wall spot (above left), for reading or focused tasks. Combine ambient and task lighting so that each fitting serves a purpose – practical yet atmospheric.

Work with Natural Light

Floor-to-ceiling glazing floods the room with soft, dappled light that moves across linen and plaster. Keep the palette tonal – chalk, oat and sand – so the light becomes the decoration. Choose a paper pendant like the Mimou Wrinkle handmade ceiling lamp to diffuse brightness and add gentle texture. Style simply: a candle, a book, a single stem in glass. When colour and proportion remain calm, natural light does the rest.

Styling with a Floral Frog

A simple decorative object can contribute to the feel of a room. Use a floral frog (a metal 'pin' style) to keep dried stems or grasses upright; it gives shape and control to loose stems. Place these in a glass vessel or decorative tray from Cooee Design, so that light can move through the form and cast soft shadows. Forage your garden for seed heads or plant clippings – their irregularity is what makes them beautiful.

The Bathroom

A bathroom is often treated as the most functional room in the house – somewhere to wash, get ready and move quickly on. In the Scandi Modern homes we visited, bathrooms became something different: retreats where surfaces and light created calm, and everyday rituals felt grounding.

In Reena's en-suite (pictured opposite), floor-to-ceiling zellige tiles transform the space. Each tile catches the light differently, the uneven glaze giving movement and depth. Texture alone can create atmosphere, even in a small room.

In Mallorca, Namali's (pages 118–35) bathroom is finished entirely in microcement. Walls, floor and basin flow together seamlessly, the continuity making the space feel sculptural yet soft. Minimal objects, natural light and linen keep it from ever feeling stark.

What these spaces showed us is that bathrooms are built on foundations you can feel: materials that add texture under hand, light that shifts from bright to soft, and simple objects that support daily ritual. These details are nothing to do with grandeur. They make bathrooms more than functional: they make them restorative.

Design for the Senses

A common theme in the Scandi Modern bathrooms we explored was the decision to begin with texture, not colour. Combine zellige tiles with polished plaster or microcement to build quiet contrast and depth. Keep grout lines fine so that surfaces read as one, and choose warm, neutral tones. Mix finishes with intention: pair matte walls with brushed brass fittings or timber shelving to balance warmth and coolness. Avoid over-lighting; fit a dimmer or low wall sconce that fades into the wall to make the bathroom feel tranquil and restorative. The goal is a bathroom that engages the senses – simple, tactile and grounding.

Style with Purpose

Built-in recesses offer space to display what matters most. Keep them purposeful: a candle on a Tine K Home or Zara Home tray, a small ceramic bowl or a vintage basket collected on your travels. Vary height and texture but leave negative space so that each piece can breathe. Group items by use – everyday toiletries together, decorative pieces apart. Choose materials that echo the architecture: plaster, stone and glass to maintain visual unity. Meaningful styling in a bathroom isn't about adding more, it's about choosing less and choosing well.

The Garden

For many years, gardens were seen as separate from the home: a lawn to mow, borders to tend, a space used only when the weather allowed. Scandi Modern takes a different approach. It treats the garden as another room of the house, lived in through the seasons, connected to daily rituals.

In the homes we visited, this was clear. Sliding doors opened wide so interiors flowed onto shaded terraces. Dining tables were laid outdoors with linen and candles, suppers stretching long into the evening. Pots of herbs clustered close to kitchens, ready to be picked and used.

In Mallorca (pages 118–35), stone floors ran straight from the living room to the terrace, climbing plants softening modern walls. Days began outside with coffee in the sun and ended under the moon, with the sound of cicadas, showing how the same Scandi Modern principles – simplicity, natural materials, atmosphere – hold true in heat as well as cold.

At Jon and Sofia's Swedish home (pages 152–65), the deck became an outdoor living room. In summer, children played until dusk while adults lingered over meals; in winter, lanterns and sheepskins kept the same terrace alive. In London, Rebecca's garden was designed to echo her interiors (pages 88–105): timber decking, planters in a muted palette, a seamless transition from inside to out. At Helena and Jakob's home (pages 166–83), terraces stepped down to a pool framed by the Gothenburg coast, used as naturally as any indoor space.

In Reena's own garden, summer evenings become ritual: pizzas cooked outside with the girls, blankets pulled across chairs as the light fades, lanterns lit one by one. It's not about grand landscaping, but about creating places in which to linger.

What we loved most about all these gardens was their ease. They don't strive for perfection. They embrace the seasons – blossom in spring, herbs in summer, branches gathered in winter. They blur boundaries, invite nature close and give families more space in which to live.

Make Space to Live Outside

Design outdoor areas as an extension of your home. Use durable materials like corten steel, timber and stone, which age well and develop character through the seasons. Ground your space with built-in planters or raised beds, to create structure and soften hard lines. A timber bench or dining table invites daily use, while a pendant or lantern brings light after dark. Even the smallest terrace can become a living space when it's designed with purpose, protected from the elements, layered with texture and made for conversation.

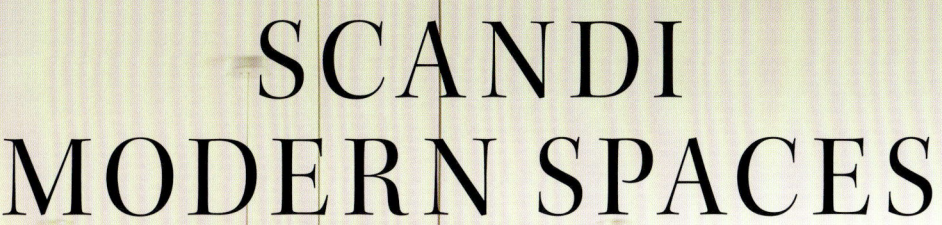

SCANDI
MODERN SPACES

THE BLACK HOUSE
IN NATURE

When Reena, her husband and their three young daughters first visited a tired 1960s bungalow nestled behind another house in Cardiff, they were immediately attracted to its quiet and private setting. Horses grazing beyond the fence and a stream running along the boundary made the space feel like a peaceful retreat, with a sense of seclusion rare in a city environment.

'We designed for light first. If we got that right, everything else could be softer.'

Reena and her family were living in a small Victorian terraced house, and Reena sensed that the bungalow represented an opportunity to create a home for their three daughters, with more space, natural light and a better flow. She envisioned a flexible home that could adapt to their family's changing needs – something she longed for.

Like many projects that were built during the pandemic, theirs unfolded in stages. Planning was complex, access was tight, supply chains were unpredictable. Looking back, Reena recognizes the delay as a gift, although at the time it was extremely stressful. 'In hindsight, it gave us time to understand the plot properly – how the sun moved, where the wind settled, the spots we naturally gravitated towards. The design sharpened because we had to wait.'

Compared to the tired bungalow they bought, the end result is unrecognizable. It has been completely transformed into a black-clad, two-storey home based around an open-plan living space, which is stitched to the garden by slim, steel-framed architectural glazing that stacks open in summer. Each glazing bar feels deliberate, framing a slightly different view,

so that every panel reads like its own picture of the garden, the water or the planting beyond. The wood exterior of this home has been charred black using a unique Japanese technique called *shou sugi ban*.

Two roof windows allow daylight to pour into the double-height plan; another, set above the staircase, draws the sky down into the space and lends the heart of the home a quiet, uplifting brightness even on grey days. 'We designed for light first. We live in rainy Wales, after all,' Reena explains. 'If we got that right, everything else could be softer.'

The kitchen anchors the main living space without dominating it. Reena favoured a timeless, crafted look over a show kitchen, choosing slim-framed inky-black cabinetry designed by Sebastian Cox for deVOL, its colour a subtle reference to the house's exterior.

Open shelves run between closed storage housing everyday ceramics and glassware. Across from the island sits a dining table, sized for real life, which Reena designed herself having been unable to find a a pre-made design she liked. It's intentionally generous: weekday homework and quick suppers at one end,

Made for Modern Living

The dining table sits at the centre of the home and has followed the family from one house to the next. Designed by Reena with local joiners, it combines a solid oak parquet top with a steel frame for strength and longevity. Slim Maxlight glazing opens the room to the garden, connecting daily life to nature and light. The matching IKEA MARKERAD chairs by Virgil Abloh balance simplicity with design integrity.

quiet laptop hours at the other, so that the space flexes with minimal resetting. 'We wanted the table to work hard,' Reena says.

Beyond the kitchen, the open-plan living space was designed as the social heart of the house. A bespoke back-to-back linen sofa designed by Reena quietly zones the room, with one side turned to the fire for quiet evenings, the other facing the garden, so that daylight and greenery remain part of daily life. It allows two moods to coexist, creating a space that is both sociable and quiet without breaking the flow of the plan.

Additional armchairs layer in flexibility, so there's always space to stretch out or draw closer together. At the centre, an oversized fireplace becomes a natural anchor in winter, its scale balancing the openness of the plan and drawing the family inwards. Because the house was essentially a new build, without the inherited character of period details, every decision here was about creating depth and atmosphere.

Materials were chosen as much for feel as for look: cross-sawn oak underfoot, polished concrete in the busiest areas and walls plastered in soft, off-white tones that shift with the light. Sheer linen curtains temper the brightness without stealing it, so daylight remains the storyteller through the day. In summer, doors fold back to the deck, where herbs and the sound of water extend the tranquil feeling of the house to the outdoors. 'For me, materiality is about how a house feels,' Reena says. 'Timber under bare feet, linen softening the light, stone that grows more beautiful with age – those details make it deeply ours.'

Half a level up, three bedrooms for the girls sit side by side – their own wing, practical and close-knit, designed for shared living as much as it is a personal space. A further half flight leads to the main suite, perched like a treehouse among the branches outside. Windows here stretch tall and slim, framing glimpses of leaves and sky. A bedroom and adjoining living space create a grown-up sanctuary, with views across the garden and stream. The en-suite continues the quiet mood, its pale finishes and simple details chosen for calm daily rituals.

'I've learnt that calm isn't the absence of stuff,' Reena says. 'It's designing so that everyday life can happen without friction.'

The garden is treated as another room, rather than as an afterthought. Planting leans textural and low-maintenance: grasses, herbs, soft greens. There's a small prep surface outside for summer suppers and a tucked-away hot tub for fine starry nights. The deck is wide enough to hold a table and a pair of chairs without feeling crowded. 'We wanted to step out and be *in it* within seconds,' Reena explains. 'No big transition – just open the doors and you're there.'

Designing her own house ignited something new for Reena: a passion for lighting and homewares that has since become part of her creative work. 'Living through the process made me realize how much atmosphere depends on the smallest details,' she explains. Rather than relying on off-the-shelf pieces, she began sketching her own ideas. A cluster of pendants now glows above the dining table, designed to feel sculptural in the day and quietly dramatic at night. In the living space, charred-wood lamps – another of her own designs – throw warm pools of light that balance the openness of the plan with intimacy.

Reena says her favourite season at The Black House is summer, when friends and her extended family gather outside and then retreat inside late at night. The spaces brim with life, sometimes so full of people it could feel like too many (Reena has six siblings, four of whom live close by) – but instead it feels exactly right. 'The house isn't precious,' Reena smiles. 'It's lived-in and loved. That's the point.'

A Place to Pause

Oak panelling from Waxed Floors' Treehouse Collection wraps select walls, adding warmth and character to the clean architectural lines. The window seat sits within that palette of natural materials – a quiet space in which to pause between indoors and out. The IKEA STOCKHOLM chairs in a bouclé fabric add affordable comfort, while a simple pine side table, also from IKEA, keeps the space feeling functional and unfussy. Though modest in scale, every detail serves a purpose, creating a calm, tactile spot for reading, coffee or simply watching light move through the trees.

Echoes of the Exterior

The kitchen takes its cue from the house's blackened timber facade, echoing the same depth of tone through its wooden cabinetry, which is stained inky-blue. Crafted in the Sebastian Cox range by deVOL, the kitchen blends natural oak with sustainable ply for quiet texture and depth. The walls are finished in a textured paint effect by Detale Copenhagen, adding soft movement and a handmade quality to the surface. A single floating shelf replaces upper units, keeping sightlines clean and open. The space feels grounded but never heavy, with natural light, Topus Concrete worktops by Caesarstone and warm brass fittings softening the darker base.

A Room Framed by Nature

The island faces the garden through full-height glazing, turning the landscape into a living artwork. Reena chose rattan stools from OKA and neutral surfaces to draw warmth into the space. It's a kitchen designed not just for cooking, but for gathering, and there is always a candle lit. The one pictured is from Loewe – a luxurious treat from a friend.

Designed to Do More

Created in collaboration with The Main Company, this multifunctional space or 'bootility', as Reena calls it, features cabinetry from Reena's own Reena Simon collection, designed to bring warmth and tactility to everyday living. Reeded rattan and fluted glass fronts soften the solid oak frames, balancing texture with light. Reena planned the layout for daily use, combining deep drawers and tall storage with a marble sink for practicality and permanence. Overhead skylights and a glazed door draw in natural light, ensuring even the hardest-working room feels peaceful, beautiful and connected to the outdoors.

Outdoor Living, Made Easy

The garden deck was designed for year-round use, creating a seamless extension of the house. The composite decking gives the look of timber but requires almost no maintenance – a practical choice for the Welsh climate. A reclaimed teak table and benches from Homebarn bring warmth and texture, while planting by Dig, with Nordic-inspired grasses and ferns, softens the edges. At the far end, a wood-clad electric hot tub offers the calm of a spa moment without the effort of wood-firing. Simple, natural and functional – it's an outdoor space made to be lived in, not just looked at.

Scandi Modern Style Moments
that define this home

THE BATHROOM AS A SANCTUARY

The family bathroom, with its textured Venetian plaster walls, generous double concrete sink and free-standing bath, invites relaxation rather than rushing. The tactility of the materials creates a spa-like atmosphere, while thoughtful design features – such as the window with adjustable privacy glass, which automatically regulates the light – enhance the sense of tranquility.

SEATING THAT FLEXES AND FLOWS

Reena's open-plan layout creates room for versatile seating solutions. Her custom-designed, back-to-back modular sofa allows the family to occupy the living space for different activities – some facing forward to watch television, while others sit away, quietly reading. Together in the same space, they can enjoy separate moments of comfort and relaxation.

GARDEN DESIGN AS INTENTIONAL AS THE INTERIOR

Gardens are often an afterthought, or, at the very least, are not spaces that feel carefully considered. By investing in features like a timber hot tub, a sunken trampoline and a spacious outdoor kitchen, Reena has created a garden that feels like a genuine extension of her home – a space where the family can relax, entertain and enjoy outdoor living to the fullest.

*'Timber under bare feet, linen softening the light,
stone that grows more beautiful with age –
those details make it deeply ours.'*

REENA'S LIFESTYLE LIST

› **Your favourite place to holiday**
Austin, Texas and New York. I love American
lake life – the stillness, the sunsets, the feeling
of space – and then the contrast of New York,
our favourite city. Its energy is unmatched;
it's electric, creative and always a lot of fun.

› **The nicest design-led accommodation
you've stayed in**
Trulli Mest'Andrea alle Lame in Noci, Italy,
is the most magical place we have ever stayed.
The interior design is divine – minimalist, with
beautifully crafted furnishings. Designed by the
husband-and-wife duo who live there, the site has
been in their family for generations. One evening,
they invited us to dinner: homemade Italian food,
their own wine and a conversation about design
translated through Google. It's a place I've never
forgotten and I'm longing to return and also visit
Masseria Calderisi next time.

› **On your playlist at home**
Ludovico Einaudi, Bon Iver or the sound of my
youngest daughter, Poppy, practising the drums.
Now that she can play with confidence, it's
become the happiest kind of background music.

› **Your go-to design read**
Elle Decoration and *Milk Magazine* – my constant
sources of inspiration and ideas.

› **Favourite ritual for unwinding**
Film nights with my three daughters; candles
glowing, blankets piled high and everyone
curled up together. It's the perfect pause at
the end of a busy week.

› **The scent that defines your home**
Loewe's 'Oregano'. I was gifted the 2-kg (4½-lb)
candle, the largest in their collection, and the
throw is incredible. It fills the whole house
with warm, woody and amber notes that feel
grounding and calming.

THE MINIMALIST FAMILY HOME

When Rebecca and her family first stepped into their 1930s home, they saw beyond its dated layout and imagined a space filled with light, warmth and flow. Moving from a narrow Edwardian terrace, they longed for a wider footprint – one that embraced Scandinavian principles of simplicity, calm and connection. 'While I loved the period features in our previous home, I welcomed the challenge of a blanker canvas, where I'd have to work harder to bring in character,' Rebecca reflects.

Her inspiration came from time spent in Denmark and Sweden, where design isn't just about aesthetics but a way of living – prioritizing natural light, a connection to nature and a mindset free from unnecessary clutter. 'It wasn't about having a perfect home, but one that felt effortless and truly lived-in.'

Like so many, the family had to press pause on their renovation plans during the pandemic. Looking back, Rebecca sees this as a blessing in disguise. 'It gave us time to really understand the space – how the light moved through the house throughout the day, where we naturally gravitated as a family.'

When renovations finally began, the family moved out, and the builders moved in. Stripping the house back to bare brick was both exciting and daunting. 'There was a terrifying moment early on when I opened the front door and realized the entire back of the house was gone. I did wonder if we'd taken on more than we could handle.'

Despite that initial panic, she trusted the process. Less than a year later, the family returned to a home transformed. At its heart is an open-plan kitchen, dining and living area – a space that brings everyone together.

Knocking down walls turned what was once a series of small, disconnected rooms into a seamless, flowing space. A statement dining table from Another Country has become the hub of daily life, functioning as a workspace, a place for slow meals with friends, and even an impromptu ping-pong table.

Storage was key in maintaining a balance between minimalism and practicality. 'With three young sons, we needed solutions that kept everyday life organized but still accessible,' says Rebecca. Built-in cabinetry, deep kitchen drawers and carefully planned shelving ensure everything has its place, helping the home feel calm without compromising on function.

The kitchen anchors the living space, with a mix of closed cabinetry and open shelving. Rebecca obsessed over the details, drawn to the simplicity of Shaker-style cabinetry but wanting a more contemporary edge. 'I couldn't find anything off-the-shelf with the narrow borders I envisioned, so I worked with a kitchen company to design bespoke cabinets,' she explains. The same cabinetry style is echoed throughout the home, creating visual continuity. Soft neutrals contrast with warmer, more tactile finishes, such as the Carrara marble worktops.

Adapting Alcoves

In the generous alcoves flanking the chimney breast of her open-plan living space, Rebecca commissioned bespoke joinery painted in Stock 37 from the Little Greene paint company. The lower cupboards echo the skinny, Shaker-style kitchen cabinetry, while open shelving above showcases carefully curated ceramics and favourite interiors books. Leaving negative space around each piece creates a calm, considered Scandi Modern feel.

'It wasn't about having a perfect home,
but one that felt effortless and truly lived-in.'

Originally, Rebecca had ruled out real marble. 'I looked at so many alternatives, but I kept coming back to the real thing. There's a softness to it that nothing else could replicate. I love that it will age and change with our home.'

Nature plays a central role in the home's aesthetic. The rear of the house overlooks mature horse chestnut trees, giving it an unexpectedly rural feel. Maximizing that connection was a priority, leading to the decision to install floor-to-ceiling glazing in the loft and large skylights that flood the interiors with natural light downstairs. The palette is intentionally muted – soft earth tones, warm oak, tactile linen, handcrafted ceramics – all working together to bring the outdoors in.

Rebecca's goal in designing the loft extension was to create a suite that recreated the nurturing feeling of staying in a luxury hotel. Separate spaces have been created for dressing, sleeping and bathing, divided by handmade screens filled with reeded glass, which blur the transitions between rooms. Rebecca credits her carpenter for this idea. 'I had originally wanted to install Crittall dividers and doors, but the quote was fairly eyewatering. My carpenter proposed making the divider from timber instead, and then we used reeded glass to give them a more expensive feel.' It's a creative solution to a cost concern that makes the space feel unique.

At the end of a busy day, the loft acts as a sanctuary: 'This is my retreat. After the chaos of family life, I unwind with a candlelit bath, embracing those slow moments that make this house feel like home.'

Now, with the renovation complete, daily rituals have taken shape. For Rebecca, it's a quiet morning cup of tea at the kitchen window, looking out onto the garden. For her husband, it's reading by the fire on winter evenings. And for their three young sons? Weekend mornings spent perched at the kitchen island, enjoying home-cooked pancakes.

Repeating Materials

Flooded with natural light from above, the dining space enjoys garden views through a generously sized window. The window seat below has built-in storage, helping to contain the chaos of family life. A dining table in pale wood from Another Country, with chairs in matching wood, echoes the kitchen detailing, subtly linking the two areas and creating a calm, cohesive flow.

Layered Texture

Leftover 'Kit Kat' tiles from the family bathroom sparked fresh inspiration for finishing the fireplace in the living space. Instead of a free-standing model, the log-burning stove is inset, creating a more streamlined, contemporary look. The Audo Copenhagen Plinth coffee table in Carrara marble introduces another material to the room, while its placement on a textured rug helps soften the space, preventing it from feeling too clinical.

A Space to Sleep

Rebecca designed three distinct zones in her loft conversion: for sleeping, bathing and dressing. The sleeping area, positioned next to floor-to-ceiling windows to maximize garden views, features a unique design detail: the light oak floorboards extend up the walls, creating a warm wooden backdrop to the spacious bed from Naturalmat, upholstered in soft bouclé fabric.

A Dream Dressing Place

The dressing area beneath the eaves has been thoughtfully designed, with custom-sized wardrobes to store the couple's clothes. To create a visual and material connection with the en-suite, Rebcca used large honed marble tiles from Mandarin Stone for the worktop in the dressing room niche. The space is finished with slimline antique brass handles from Corston Architectural, similar to the style seen in the downstairs kitchen, which add a warm metallic touch.

Clean Lines, Quiet Luxury

The en-suite bathroom was designed around the placement, by the window, of a luxurious free-standing bath with accompanying brass-finish, free-standing mixer tap. Soft linen blinds from Silent Gliss, operated by remote control, provide privacy without compromising quality of light. Choosing to forgo a traditional glass screen, Rebecca instead created a bespoke, curved shower enclosure, finished in the same warm-beige Festfloor microcement as the walls.

Scandi Modern Style Moments
that define this home

LIGHT AS A DESIGN TOOL

The house was restructured to maximize daylight, removing barriers that blocked the flow of light between rooms. Two large rooflights now flood the kitchen with natural light, and floor-to-ceiling glazing in the loft creates an uninterrupted connection to the outdoors.

A NEUTRAL BUT LAYERED PALETTE

A base of soft off-whites and warm beige tones keeps the space serene, with materials like light oak flooring and honed Carrara marble adding depth. Rather than bold contrasts, the design relies on tonal variation and subtle shifts in texture to create interest.

INTEGRATED STORAGE FOR A CLEAN AESTHETIC

The key to maintaining Scandi Modern simplicity in a family home is designing storage solutions that allow for daily life to happen without visual clutter. However much storage you think you need at the outset, add more! Custom cabinetry in the living area ensures that books, games and essentials have a home, while in the kitchen, deep drawers and built-in shelving make it easy to maintain order.

> *A base of soft off-whites and warm beige tones keeps the space serene, with materials like light oak flooring and honed Carrara marble adding depth.*

REBECCA'S LIFESTYLE LIST

> **Your favourite place to holiday**

Fredriksberg in Copenhagen – a family-friendly neighbourhood – followed by languid days in Tisvilde (the 'Danish Hamptons'). I love picking up fresh cinnamon buns from local bakeries, relaxing on the beach and winding down on the terrace of the Helenekilde hotel.

> **The nicest design-led accommodation you've stayed in**

The 1 Hotel Brooklyn – offering breathtaking views, *hygge* interiors and a signature candle that fills the air with a divine scent.

> **On your playlist at home**

The soothing sounds of The National, Sam Fender, Radiohead, This Is The Kit and Ben Howard often set the mood.

> **Your go-to design read**

Enki magazine, which combines inspiring architecture, minimal interiors and lifestyle ideas. I eagerly anticipate each month's edition.

> **Favourite ritual for unwinding**

A long, luxurious bath – warm water, soft lighting, a flickering candle and bath salts from Bamford to melt away the tensions of the week.

> **The scent that defines your home**

The woody green notes of the Aesop 'Callippus' candle, which defines the atmosphere of my home. I stockpile them just in case it's ever discontinued!

THE MAXIMALIST TOWNHOUSE

'Eclectic, elegant and calm' are the three words Elle King, Design Director of Ett Hem London, uses to describe the East London home she shares with her Swedish husband Robin, stepson Alex and their Golden Retriever Max.

'Scandi design can be bold and textured. I love the combination of high-end materials – wood, marble and metal. Not everything is vanilla clean lines.'

The four-storey period maisonette sits a short walk from London Fields, an East London neighbourhood that attracts many creatives. The Scandi–British couple previously lived in west London, around Notting Hill and Holland Park, before succumbing to the pull of the east: 'The undeniably cooler side of London; where trends are made, restaurants are born and cocktail bars buzz late into the night,' as Elle describes it.

When they first viewed the property it was run-down, but the couple immediately saw its potential. High ceilings, light-filled rooms and original period details, including large sash windows, were the key selling points.

Their home reflects both of their cultures, with Scandinavian simplicity meeting British tradition. 'It's a calm but considered space,' Elle explains. 'Primarily it's our safe home, but it's also a creative space to develop my business, Ett Hem London, which creates curated faux floral arrangements.'

We loved how Elle had woven these floral creations into her own interior: for example, an arrangement of tulips was given elevated staus in the dining room by being placed on a pedestal – a clever way to play with scale to create visual interest in the room.

Plants and greenery are prominent in Elle's home beyond these floral designs. Black Crittall-style doors fold open across the rear of the house to reveal an unexpected oasis: established olive, bay and magnolia trees, banana and pear trees, a lemon tree and a huge wisteria. 'They need a lot of pruning, but they're a beloved feature,' Elle says. In spring the wisteria wraps the balcony and floods the kitchen with its heady scent.

The kitchen walls are painted a soft beige that creates a Scandi Modern backdrop for the showpiece: a striking Viola marble waterfall island and splashback, set off by deep, inky-blue cabinets. When evening falls, a sculptural light – the Audo Copenhagen TR Bulb Suspension Frame pendant – casts a warm glow over the island. Robin is the chef and takes charge of cooking and cocktails, while Elle curates the table and atmosphere.

Lighting that Makes a Statement

The couple have created a luxurious bathroom centred around a vintage roll-top bath. Overhead, a Flos 2097 chandelier by Gino Sarfatti adds a sculptural focal point – a nod to their love of mid-century design classics.

One level up, the dining room has hosted many dinner parties. '"Galentines" has to be my favourite occasion to host,' Elle says. 'The flowers, the tablescape, the guests and the music make it perfect.' Iconic Scandinavian pieces – a tulip-style table, sculptural dining chairs and a leather sling chair tucked into a corner – reinforce the design sensibility, while a pink glass chandelier from Pure White Lines adds the bold, British counterpoint that has become the couple's signature.

While Robin is the native Swede, Elle admits she's the one most drawn to Scandinavian style. But she rejects the notion that Scandi design must be minimalist: 'It can be bold and textured. I love the combination of high-end materials – wood, marble and metal. Not everything is vanilla clean lines.' Robin, by contrast, leans maximalist: the third-floor living room showcases his collection of fashion books, combined with the couple's eclectic art pieces. 'We have lots of art in the house – everything has emotional value. We buy it because we love it,' Elle says. Several pieces hold a particularly personal significance: works by Elle's parents – her mother, a ceramicist, and her father, a photographer – are dotted through the house.

The vintage mid-century sideboard in the dining room is just one of the Scandinavian classics Robin has painstakingly sourced from eBay. 'I like to think the furniture brings a story with it,' he says. 'It's also more sustainable than buying new.' At the top of their furniture wish list is a design classic by Børge Mogensen – the Spanish chair, designed for Fredericia in 1958. 'They're incredibly hard to find, and often more expensive second-hand than brand new,' Elle explains.

With renovations complete on three of the four floors, only the loft remains to be transformed. 'We've stayed true to the original layout, and every room has a different purpose, which, on reflection, is exactly why we love the house,' Elle says.

Though they might one day move back west in search of a bigger house and more outdoor space for entertaining, for now the family are happily rooted in the gentle rhythms and daily rituals of their East London home. At the weekend they walk Max through London Fields, pick up ingredients from nearby Broadway Market, and prepare lunch around the kitchen island before eating outside in the garden, surrounded by trees, soaking up the feeling of calm despite the bustle of London just moments away.

A Room for Rituals

Elle celebrates the dining room's role in gathering friends together, with her playlists setting the mood. The vintage tulip table perfectly contrasts with the British period details, blending Scandi style with classic charm.

Scandi Modern Style Moments
that define this home

MATERIAL-LED LUXURY

A neutral, Scandinavian-inspired style is elevated by the addition of luxurious textures – simple lines are paired with rich and tactile surfaces that add depth to the space. In the kitchen, painting the walls in a soft, buttery beige allows the Viola marble waterfall island, inky-blue cabinets and warm wood accents to come together as one, vibrant whole.

LAYERED LIVING

Unlike some of the more contemporary Scandinavian homes we visited, Elle and Robin's home separates functions carefully by level and layer, with spaces thoughtfully connected rather than merged into one open plan. While many might see walls as barriers to connection, the couple have embraced the separation of spaces, using it to create cosy, cocooning environments with a sense of retreat and intimacy.

CURATED CLASSICS
WITH PERSONAL HEART

Vintage Scandinavian pieces, family artworks and carefully sourced accents give the rooms character and story. From eBay-sourced mid-century sideboards to faux-floral designs by Elle's own brand, Ett Hem London, the look feels collected not contrived – timeless, sustainable and warmly personal.

'We have lots of art in the house – everything has emotional value. We buy it because we love it.'

ELLE'S LIFESTYLE LIST

❯ Your favourite place to holiday

Europe in spring and fall – West Ibiza, North Mallorca, Tuscany, the South of France; I also love Cape Town during the winter. For design inspiration, Milan, Florence and Stockholm are my favourites for their timeless yet modern appeal. They offer exhibitions, concept stores and great restaurants, without any jet lag.

❯ The nicest design-led accommodation you've stayed in

La Fiermontina in Lecce, with its art gallery suite – a unique space that combines elegance, art and comfort. Other favourites include Palazzo Daniele, Reschio, The Venice Venice Hotel and Le Sirenuse in Positano.

❯ On your playlist at home

A mix of jazz and diverse genres, shaped by my background in a family connected to the music industry. It's about moods and moments – whatever feels right; music is an incredibly important part of our home life.

❯ Your go-to design read

For design inspiration, our go-to spot is the Broadway Market bookshop. We love the tactile experience of flipping through incredible publications. Robin is a collector of fashion books, but we've had to put a pause on it until we can find more space for them all!

❯ Favourite ritual for unwinding

My favourite ritual at home is actually how our days begin. Mornings start with Robin brewing fresh coffee from Allpress London beans; it's served upstairs for a quiet, connected beginning to the day.

❯ The scent that defines your home

The Nue Co's 'Functional Fragrance' is a calming, versatile scent that lends tranquility to our living space. I use it on myself, around the house and even on our flowers. I truly can't live without it.

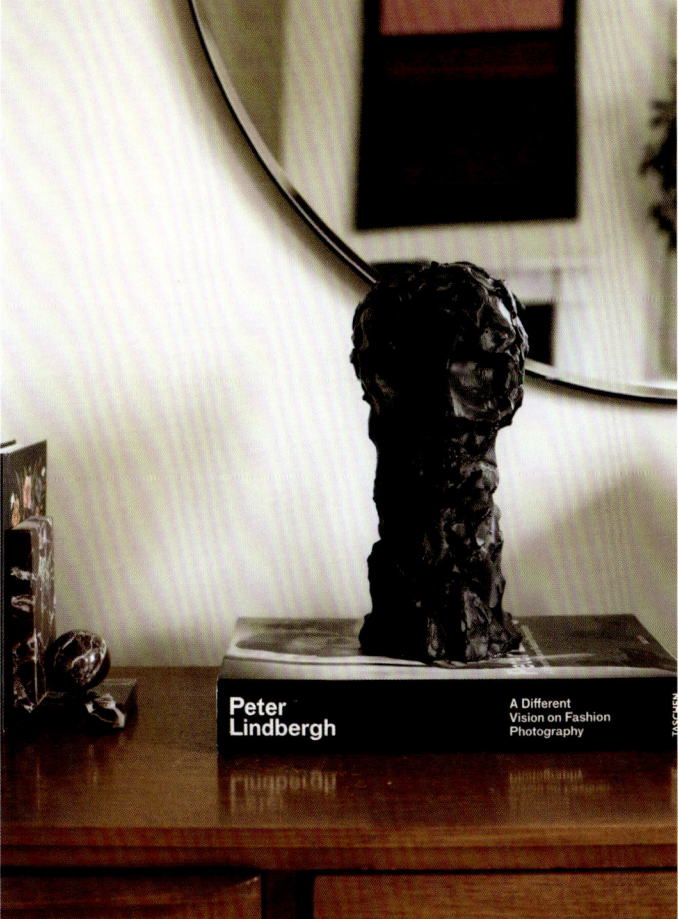

Peter
Lindbergh

A Different
Vision on Fashion
Photography

OPENHOUSE

SCANDIRUSTIC

THE ISLAND
RESIDENCE

A chance meeting in a Palma café kindled a love story that led Namali Schleberger to trade life in Germany for Mallorca's luminous landscapes. She had come to the island from Munich for a two-month interlude, renting an apartment for herself and her two young children. One morning, while seeking the familiar comfort of her coffee ritual, she struck up conversation with Linus, a retired Tour de France rider who had moved to the island after retiring from cycling. He had made his home in Deià, a jewel-like mountaintop village perched between craggy peaks and turquoise coves.

High–Low Style

In the soaring living space, two abstract artworks by Joan Bennassar on either side of the chimney breast command attention. These investment pieces are balanced by tactile elements, like the concrete-effect side table and a vase of olive branches pulled from the garden, thoughtfully curated under Namali's discerning eye.

When the gates swing open, a dwelling is revealed that looks as if it has always belonged to the island, while, inside, soft luxuries effortlessly support modern living.

Three weeks after that chance meeting, Namali explains, 'I abandoned any thought of returning home', starting a new life in Deià instead.

Born in Sri Lanka to a German father and a Sri Lankan mother, Namali recalls growing up in a house that was well known in Colombo, its big table constantly surrounded by friends from around the world. That love of gathering stayed with her and planted the seed for her first venture on the island: the restaurant, Nama. 'I always felt that having a restaurant would be like opening the door to our home,' she says. 'Although I knew nothing about the world of food and drink – my background was in television – I just knew I wanted to give something back to Deià, which had given me so much.'

The restaurant grew from an abandoned townhouse that Linus and Namali painstakingly restored, working closely with local artisans to revive original features, such as an olive-trunk roof. As Nama quickly became an established part of village life, its large communal table sparking the same conversations and connections Namali remembers from Colombo, the couple began to turn their thoughts to new adventures.

On his rides around the island, Linus found himself increasingly drawn to the quiet countryside around Binissalem, and the idea of building their own home there took root. 'I knew there was a special opportunity to create a property that could sit in harmony with the island's nature,' he explains. 'We didn't just want to build a house; we wanted to create a home.'

Working with local architects, artisans and builders, they have made something truly

special that draws strongly on Scandinavian design principles. From the road, the house is concealed behind gates of solid oak; when those gates swing open, a dwelling is revealed that looks as if it has always belonged to the island, while inside, soft luxuries effortlessly support modern living.

On either side of the house, views of the surrounding landscape (including the rugged Tramuntana mountains) are framed by soaring Crittall windows and doors; their slim steel frames provide a modern counterpoint to the rough-hewn local stone in which they sit.

At the heart of the home, a generous open-plan kitchen and living area unfolds, anchored of course by a large dining table, around which family and friends can gather.

Scandi Modern principles guide the interior: soft neutrals and natural materials are used, which echo the outside. Reclaimed timber cabinets and smooth concrete worktops give the kitchen an earthy, grounded feel under its soaring ceilings. Open shelving along the back wall holds carefully curated objects that spark conversation. This is a kitchen designed to foster connection. During our visit we gathered around the reclaimed wooden dining table beneath a trio of rattan pendants as Namali prepared pizzas, crafting a simple, delicious lunch from local ingredients.

Some might have been daunted by the challenge of making the large living space feel cosy, but, through Namali's careful layering of textures and thoughtful seating plan, a *hygge* warmth pervades. Anchored by a soaring chimney breast – its smooth plaster finish set against a rugged stone hearth – two large linen sofas invite you to sink down and pause for a while.

Perhaps the space works so well because of Namali's previous career in TV production and her eye for setting a stage. 'I'm a very visual person,' she says with a smile. 'I always think in terms of cameras, so everything in a room has to conjure a good feeling and every perspective must be perfect. When you enter a room creating emotion is the most important thing – it's exactly the same in TV.'

The furniture choices are a clever mix of high and low, with lamps, woven-back chairs and side tables sourced from Zara blending seamlessly with more expensive pieces, such as the sofas in a rich chocolate-brown linen from Spanish design brand By Blasco. What makes the space feel truly personal, though, is the collection of large scale artworks that adorn the walls. The collection includes pieces by local artists such as Joan Bennàssar and Heinz Ackermann, as well as international artists carefully curated by Namali's friend and art advisor Patrice Farameh.

Two wings of bedrooms and bathrooms flank the central living space. To the left, a luxurious suite for Namali and Linus: a sunlit bedroom with a cosy seating nook, a thoughtfully arranged dressing room and a generous en-suite, where pale microcement walls and soft light create a private sanctuary.

In both the bedroom and the bathroom Namali has recessed shelving niches into the walls, which function as small gallery spaces, containing personal photographs and objects, contemporary ceramics and objects that bring her Sri Lankan heritage into the Scandi Modern interior. In one of the bathroom niches a small Buddha is backlit, lending a quietly spiritual air to bathing rituals, while the window frames olive branches stirring in the breeze.

A quiet intent threads throughout the interior: nothing is excessive, everything chosen with care. This approach carries into Namali's daughter's room, where a canvas in pale pink tones drifts above the bed, adding a gentle, feminine echo to the room.

The couple's vision for their own home has now translated into a new venture together: Soul Escapes – a collection of carefully designed and crafted properties, located in the green valleys of Valdemossa and in the countryside that surrounds their own plot. 'Much as in our own home, we want to create spaces that are in harmony with their surroundings, choosing local products and finishes that complement the island's natural beauty.'

A Sense of Place

The couple prioritized locally sourced materials in their interior design, fostering a deeper connection to the region. In the kitchen, the striking island is crafted from locally sourced stone, adding both authenticity and a sense of place to the room.

Think Niche

Namali's Sri Lankan heritage comes through strongly in the bedroom, where she planned wall niches behind the bed that create space for carefully curated displays of treasured family photos and objects with personal meaning. The items selected for display have a cohesive, rich, earthy colour palette.

A Spa-like Feeling

The spacious en-suite that leads from the couple's bedroom looks out over the gardens, so long soaks in the bath are accompanied by garden views. Here, again, Namali has cleverly added niches to the wall, where art and objects are displayed; these elevate the bathroom from being a purely functional space to a more personal, even spiritual one.

Pergola Moments

To the west of the house, a swimming pool sits subtly disguised by the Mediterranean planting design. After long hot days by the pool, the couple enjoy hosting friends under the pergola for meals cooked in the outdoor kitchen. Statement rattan pendant lights illuminate outdoor gatherings late into the Mallorcan night.

Home Among the Hills

The couple called upon renowned Spanish landscape artist Álvaro Sampedro to design the expansive gardens that surround the house. Known for his forward thinking, nature-led approach, he has used plants native to the island to weave Namali and Linus's house into the surrounding landscape.

Scandi Modern Style Moments
that define this home

ARCHITECTURAL FRAMES FOR BREATHTAKING VIEWS

Sleek, slim steel Crittall windows and doors serve as modern art pieces in their own right, seamlessly connecting the interior with spectacular vistas of the Tramuntana mountains and olive groves, blurring the boundary between home and landscape.

THE ART OF MIXING HIGH WITH LOW

Having invested in high-quality materials for the foundations of their home, Namali and Linus cleverly incorporated accessible, high-street pieces into their interior. Lamps and a rough linen throw in the bedroom, and a creamy microcement side table and vase in the living room, were all sourced from Zara Home.

DISPLAY WITH DEPTH

Whether designing a new home or renovating an existing space, consider incorporating wall niches into your plans. These recessed spaces, like the ones in Namali's bedroom and bathroom, create beautiful opportunities for adding depth and personality to your interiors.

'I knew there was an opportunity to create a property that could sit in harmony with the island's nature … We didn't just want to build a house, we wanted to create a home.'

› **Your favourite place to holiday**

Mallorca, our beloved island for staycations – full of undiscovered treasures – and further afield, South Africa, especially Cape Town, with its stunning landscapes. Sri Lanka is also special, with a strong personal connection. It's wonderful to see more visitors discovering its unique appeal now.

› **The nicest design-led accommodation you've stayed in**

Private rentals via Airbnb. Recommendations from Mr and Mrs Smith or Pretty Hotels have also led us to some incredible places. I hope one day to visit Reschio in Umbria, set among vineyards, lakes and olive groves, for ultimate relaxation.

› **On your playlist at home**

Soul and funk provide the groove, while Ludovico Einaudi and The Cinematic Orchestra offer calming soundscapes that create a perfect atmosphere for us to unwind.

› **Your go-to design read**

Architectural Digest and my collection of books on Lautner, Zaha Hadid and Mies van der Rohe keep my creative ideas flowing.

› **Favourite ritual for unwinding**

Sitting in our beautiful garden designed by the talented Spanish landscape architect Álvaro Sampedro, listening to the birds and looking at the natural beauty around us with all the butterflies and bees flying around. A simple pleasure that fills my heart with joy.

› **The scent that defines your home**

Pot Pourri from Officina Profumo-Farmaceutica di Santa Maria Novella from Florence – the natural scent makes you want to wind down.

THE CREATIVE QUARTERS

'Every home holds its own life.' That core belief has guided Norwegian couple Kine and Kristoffer as they shaped both their family home and their design studio, Ask og Eng. 'Ask og Eng began from a personal need,' Kine explains. 'We were looking for a kitchen that reflected who we are – our values as much as our aesthetic: sustainable, functional and beautiful.'

What started as a shared project grew into a business, and, over time, into a brand, housed at first in their Oslo home and a nearby workshop. After several client projects brought them to the Spanish island of Mallorca, however, the couple found themselves seduced by the island's light and slower pace. They imagined a new chapter shaped by softer skies, different seasons and a lifestyle more attuned to outdoor living.

Today their workshop remains in Oslo but their design studio is tucked into a narrow townhouse in Binissalem, where work and family life with their two young sons overlap. Local textures, artisanal materials and the region's warm light spark inspiration for their projects. 'Our work has always come from how we want to live,' Kine says. 'Here, that is clearer than ever.'

Their first home on Mallorca was not the townhouse in Binissalem but a rural finca with thick stone walls and sweeping views over olive groves. It gave the family the quiet and space they needed to settle in, but the finca also revealed a truth: total seclusion wasn't for them. As Kine reflects, 'balance matters'. In Binissalem they are closer to the boys' schools and within easier reach of Palma.

Of the house they have chosen as their base, Kine explains, 'we were looking for something real, and with potential, that had a quiet sense of place.' Stepping inside from winding streets of honey-coloured houses you are immediately met by a sense of calm. The entrance functions as both threshold and manifesto: a hint of the Scandi Modern aesthetic that runs through the entire home. 'We try to blend Scandinavian clarity with the warmth of other influences: light textures, natural materials, minimal lines, but full of soul,' Kristoffer explains.

Because the house is rented, they couldn't alter the structure or repaint the walls, so they focused on surface and atmosphere instead. Custom furniture, layered textiles and carefully chosen objects transform the rooms, creating a lived-in mood that feels intentional, not staged. Many of the furniture pieces are free-standing – a deliberate choice, Kine says, that 'gives more freedom and air, and not just in rentals'.

The upper floor, where the bedrooms and bathroom sit, is reserved purely for family life; downstairs doubles as both home and creative studio – a space Kine hopes 'feels warm and welcoming, not just for us but for anyone who steps inside'.

Lighting is integral to this atmosphere. The couple began by studying the natural light, then layered in lamps and low-level sources of light to build warmth and shadow, deliberately avoiding harsh ceiling spots in favour of mood and depth. And while white walls can read as cold in some interiors, here they act as a quiet backdrop, allowing personal treasures to speak: wall pieces made from clay during a family trip to Japan, ceramics gifted by a Norwegian friend and objects the pair have designed themselves.

Texture provides further depth. 'We combine rough with smooth, bamboo with stone, linen with ceramics, so nothing feels flat or over-designed,' Kine say. This method keeps the scheme minimal yet tactile, refined yet human. Material honesty, simplicity, and the idea of

Sustainable Materials

Kine and Kristoffer have designed free-standing furniture made from bamboo to fill the showroom area of their space. Their choice of material reflects a commitment to sustainability, as bamboo is a rapidly growing, renewable resource that minimizes environmental impact.

'We try to blend Scandinavian clarity with the warmth of other influences: light textures, natural materials, minimal lines, but full of soul.'

not using more than is needed are values that resonate deeply with the couple, along with a shared love of nature. Kine explains how nature is everywhere in their home, 'through the windows, in the light, in the handmade objects and materials we live with.'

It is the natural setting of the island that they treasure – its atmosphere, the surrounding mountains, the kindness of neighbours, the rural landscape, the smell of citrus trees in spring. During our own visit, we noticed how it invited us to slow down and notice everything.

Perhaps Kine puts it best when she says: 'While everyday life here isn't a holiday, there's something about it that can make an ordinary Wednesday feel like a taste of freedom. A pizza by the beach and a swim after school and work feel pretty special.'

They have settled into new routines and rhythms: coffee after the school run is sacred; days and evenings are about checking in, with each other or with their team. 'Drawing, writing,

walking. Our work and family life overlap, and we try to let that be a strength,' says Kristoffer. Weekends start with slow brunches, time to create or think while the boys play in the turquoise waters of their pool. Afterwards, a walk through the neighbourhood, then dinner in the courtyard with friends. For Kine the best gatherings are 'always informal. Shared food, open doors, Kristoffer's cocktails by the pool with no end time.'

The couple didn't arrive with a plan, just an openess to exploring how the island could fit into their lives, and slowly Mallorca opened something in them, moving them to stay.

The house in Binassalem is not their final resting point – their dream is to one day create something more from scratch and completely designed by them, whether that is a new-build or renovation of an older building. 'We have ideas, but we're not rushing. We're letting the island and possibilities guide us . . . we imagine it will,' says Kine.

Elevating the Everyday

The floor-to-ceiling cabinet in the showroom showcases a curated mix of material samples, ceramic objects designed by the couple and practical items like balls of twine and scissors. Each object is thoughtfully displayed, so that everyday items are elevated into artful compositions.

Quiet Entrances

As you step off a busy Binissalem street and into the couple's home, a sense of tranquility instantly envelops you. White walls provide a serene backdrop to textured artworks, while wall-mounted drawers discreetly store the clutter of family life. A single, simple stem of natural grass in a wooden flower frog adds a touch of calm.

Designing the Outdoors

The couple have extended the design language of the interior out to the exterior, where a sleek, linear swimming pool takes centre stage. Beds of natural grasses edged in corten steel create a modern garden ambience, which can be enjoyed from the bamboo benches placed outside. On hot summer days, a gently fringed parasol provides welcome relief from the sun.

Scandi Modern Style Moments
that define this home

BLENDING OF FUNCTION AND ATMOSPHERE

The decision to use free standing furniture and focus on surface and atmosphere rather than structural changes reflects a Scandi Modern approach. It emphasizes flexibility, beauty and the importance of a welcoming environment that feels personalized and lived-in, even in a rental property.

MAKING SPACE MATTER

Although the townhouse was narrow in dimension, Kristoffer and Kine made it feel more expansive through their choice of white walls and clean lines, maximizing the amount of natural light available.

OUTDOOR FURNITURE AS A THOUGHTFUL DESIGN ELEMENT

The couple approached their outdoor space with intention, choosing textured materials like corten steel and bamboo to add contrast and interest. Their choices served as an extension of their interior style, enhancing the overall atmosphere.

'While everyday life here isn't a holiday, there's something about it that can make an ordinary Wednesday feel like a taste of freedom.'

KINE & KRISTOFFER'S LIFESTYLE LIST

> **Your favourite place to holiday**

The Balearics – their pristine beaches, lush nature and vibrant culture make the islands an ideal place to relax and unwind.

> **The nicest design-led accommodation you've stayed in**

Maana Homes in Kyoto – an amazing retreat blending tradition with contemporary comfort. Another inspiring experience was Hosinoya in Tokyo, perfect for a honeymoon. For a special treat, Six Senses Ibiza and Zulu in Zanzibar are unforgettable destinations.

> **On your playlist at home**

Our tastes are broad, ranging from indie rock – SYML, Girl in Red, The National, Wilco and The Decemberists – to Latin rhythms from Hermanos Gutiérrez and Karol G.

> **Your go-to design read**

Norwegian design magazine *Nytt Rom* is a source of inspiration that captures modern Scandinavian style and connects us to home.

> **Favourite ritual for unwinding**

Time in our garden at sunset, lighting candle lanterns and breathing in the Mediterranean air, with soft music playing and perhaps a glass of wine.

> **The scent that defines your home**

Smoked lavender, which has become a favourite. We grow it in our backyard and often bring the scent indoors, creating a relaxed and aromatic atmosphere.

THE HOME
BY THE SEA

After a decade of soaking up Stockholm's energy and culture, Jon and Sofia Flobrant felt a gentler call: to family and roots. Together with their young son, they returned to Kalmar, the southeastern town on the Baltic Sea where they both grew up. 'Light here has a different quality – softer, salt-tinted. The pace of life is slower,' Sofia says.

Once Jon and Sofia decided to move back to Kalmar, the house hunt began – and serendipity did the rest. A chance conversation with a neighbour led Sofia's mother to a plot of available land, just 500 yards from her own front door in Dunö.

The plot, at the very tip of a wooded peninsula and surrounded by trees, was being carved from the garden of a local resident, Stig, who owned one of the oldest homes on the island. As he reached one hundred years old, the garden had become too much for him to tend, and he was willing to sell a section suitable for building.

Although they faced fierce competition for the corner site – prized for its direct sea views – Stig ultimately chose the Flobrants, as, Sofia says, he 'wanted to entrust the land to a young family starting out life together.'

Having succeeded in securing the plot, the couple brought Hem1 on board (a company that offers architectural services and full turnkey construction) to design a house that would make the most of its location. The result is a striking, timber-clad home that spans the site, its warm wooden facade intended to weather gently and merge into the surrounding landscape over time. Sofia says, 'we wanted it to feel lived-in and open for gatherings. We paid a lot of attention to natural light and the views.'

Inside, the layout is carefully arranged to capture natural daylight. At the heart of the home, a central living space is flooded with light from large picture windows on two sides, which frame the views and create an airy, panoramic room, blurring the line between indoors and out.

Sofia's role as Head of Social Media and Affiliate Marketing at Nordic Nest – a Swedish retailer specializing in Scandinavian design – has given her a sharp eye for interiors, so it's no surprise that both traditional and contemporary Nordic brands appear throughout the house. In the living room, two armchairs anchor the space – one a vintage Jetson chair by Bruno Mathsson, the other a Laminett chair by Swedese – their sculptural silhouettes providing a focal point.

While Swedish and Danish design classics furnish the house, what truly sets Jon and Sofia's home apart is how they've woven treasured family heirlooms into the Scandi Modern scheme. When her grandmother downsized, Sofia explains that she 'rescued an old display cabinet and then stripped it back to bare wood and repainted it a soft, primrose yellow,' an intervention that makes the piece read as deliberate rather than merely inherited. Its shelves stage a quiet dialogue between past and present: her grandmother's pewter candlesticks sit beside scented candles from &Tradition, while time-worn ceramic jugs share a shelf with more contemporary finds.

On the couple's burled walnut coffee table rests a book with further personal resonance. 'As a keen photographer, it has long been my dream to author a book,' Jon explains. With creative friends Jacob and Fredrik, that ambition became reality: together they produced a striking visual guide to Öland, a nearby island. In the book, Jon's raw, atmospheric landscape photography is paired with intimate portraits and first-hand stories from the people who have shaped the place, past and present.

Design Classics Light the Room

In the living space, concrete floors pair beautifully with natural timber-framed windows, transforming each view into a living piece of art. A vintage Jetson armchair by Bruno Mathsson, won at auction the year Sofia turned 30, takes pride of place by the window. The large arc light is the iconic Arco lamp by Flos, while the ceiling pendant is the Dancing pendant from Audo Copenhagen.

'Our home is a place to exhale – a space for all of us to feel at ease and spend time together.'

Within the dining space of their home the couple are shaping their own stories; with their family growing from one son to two and relatives nearby, mealtimes are often multigenerational. The dining table they selected – the Mi 901 by Bruno Mathsson – comfortably seats a crowd, while a large picture window provides a changing backdrop: the tree outside changes with the seasons, framing dinnertime conversations with a quietly cinematic rhythm.

In the summer months, timber-framed doors slide back and the generous deck becomes a true extension of the living space. During our visit the boys arrived home, flung off their bags and raced outside to play, later settling for a casual dinner at the round table outside, shaded from the afternoon sun by a striped parasol.

For larger gatherings, Jon and Sofia favour the decking to the other side of the house, where they've hung delicate strings of lights that throw a warm, convivial glow as dusk falls, turning the area into an intimate al fresco room for long summer evenings with friends.

Jon and Sofia's ground-floor bedroom overlooks the deck, and as the sun slides west across the house, late light fractures across the bedroom's pale walls, throwing dappled shadows. At the foot of the couple's bed, an IKEA bench holds cosy sheepskin slippers for colder months;

a small stack of interiors and photography books sits on top, for bedtime reading.

Upstairs the boys have carved out their own part of the house, with two bedrooms connected by a play area. 'Our home is a place to exhale – a space for all of us to feel at ease and spend time together. The upstairs belongs to the kids, giving them freedom to play. Downstairs we try to keep things a little tidier.'

With the main house interior now complete, the couple have turned their attention to finishing the guest annex so that they can host more friends from their Stockholm life. 'It's fully clad in plywood,' explains Sofia, which gives it a warm natural feel while allowing it to blend in beautifully with the surroundings. Outside the annex, Sofia says, 'we're thinking of perhaps adding a pergola to create shaded seating.'

There is no rush to their plans – the island has worked its magic, slowing the pace of life. Long summer days start with breakfast on their terrace while the boys enjoy running around the garden. Later, the family venture out through the surrounding woods, walking down to the nearby jetty for swims or exploring the small beaches that ring the shore.

Winter brings a different kind of wonder: the water sometimes freezes solid enough to skate and new memories are made on the ice.

Contrasting Colours

While the overall backdrop of their home remains neutral, Sofia likes to introduce subtle touches of contrasting colour in earthy tones. For instance, in the bedroom, two pillowcases with a russet stripe serve as a subtle focal point on the bed.

Scandi Modern Style Moments
that define this home

DESIGN IN DIALOGUE WITH NATURE

Materials have been selected that harmonize with the landscape rather than competing with it. The timber cladding, used across both the facade and roof, is a clever choice because it will gradually weather with time, shifting in tone and character. Depending on the time of day and quality of light, it reveals a spectrum of shades.

USING THE LANDSCAPE AS ART

With panoramic views on all sides, keeping the interior walls deliberately minimal (instead of filling them with artwork) draws the eye to the landscape beyond, with large picture windows strategically placed to frame views that change with the season.

CREATING A HOME WOVEN WITH HISTORY

Incorporating meaningful pieces with personal history into their interior design added a deep sense of emotion to Jon and Sofia's newly built home. Heirlooms can be refreshed, as Sofia did by painting her grandmother's cabinet in a modern hue. Blending vintage objects with contemporary finds creates spaces imbued with feeling.

'Light here has a different quality – softer, salt-tinted. The pace of life is slower.'

❯ Your favourite place to holiday

As lovers of active holidays, we would always choose a ski trip over a relaxing beach vacation. The Swedish mountains are truly magical in winter, and in summer we love to explore the Alps or the Swedish fjällen, surrounded by nature's breathtaking scenery.

❯ The nicest design-led accommodation you've stayed in

Yasuragi Spa Hotel in Stockholm has been a lifelong inspiration – its seamless blend of nature and interiors has influenced the design of our own home, creating a calming and organic environment.

❯ On your playlist at home

Our playlists shift with our moods. We enjoy a mix of hip hop and jazz. Swedish artists like Dina Ögon, Fricky, Hannes and Junior Brielle often feature in the soundtrack of our everyday life.

❯ Your go-to design read

While most of our ideas come from social media – Pinterest and Instagram boards – we still cherish flipping through magazines. Every now and then we subscribe to interior design magazines for that tactile, inspiring experience.

❯ Favourite ritual for unwinding

On Fridays, we come home and cook together as a family, put on some music and relax on the sofa – our favourite way to unwind. We also love slow weekend mornings: buying fresh bread, brewing endless pots of coffee, opening the patio doors and planning the days ahead.

❯ The scent that defines your home

We love the scent of wood, tar and citrus. When our house was newly built, the smell of fresh timber filling every room was pure bliss, creating a natural and comforting atmosphere.

THE HOUSE UPON
THE ROCKS

While walking near their home in the Gothenburg suburbs, Helena and Jakob Bundgaard would often notice a forlorn house set back from the road. Perched on a small rise, it commanded sweeping views across the archipelago – a scatter of tiny islands dissolving into the horizon – but it had been allowed to go to ruin.

After hundreds of walks past the site, a small notice in the local paper caught their eye: the plot was for sale. Recognizing the ruined house and its extraordinary outlook, they knew instantly they would make an offer – despite having no previous plans to buy land or build. 'We had no clear idea of the kind of house we wanted to create,' Helena admits. 'We just knew that this was the place.'

Having secured the plot, they worked with a talented local architect to conceive a black-clad house of clean lines and purposeful simplicity – spare in form but rich in atmosphere.

The inspiration for the interior began with the kitchen. 'We love cooking and spending time in the kitchen, so it naturally became the main focus during the build,' Helena says. 'We even contacted our kitchen supplier before choosing a construction company.' From that starting point the home's material palette and design language took shape: a restrained aesthetic grounded in tactile detail.

'We wanted the house to embody functionalism and minimalism – but never at the expense of comfort,' Helena adds. 'It was important that the space didn't feel sterile. Our aim was a thoughtful balance of minimalism, functionality and *hygge*.' Material choices were central to that aim: limestone, pale wood, linen and leather introduce calm, layered, organic texture. Walls and furnishings settle into a soft, earthy palette of beige and brown, creating a serene, cohesive backdrop.

A strong connection to nature underpinned their Scandi Modern vision. 'We wanted the house to blend seamlessly into its surroundings – both the neighbouring architecture and the landscape,' Helena explains. Crittall-style windows are carefully sited to frame the pine trees, rocky outcrops and swathes of blooming heather beyond, so the views become part of the interior.

The outdoor spaces were choreographed around the sun: a pool tucked at the back drinks in the morning light, while expansive front decking offers a place to dine and linger as the day softens.

Helena describes how the outdoor space shapes family life: 'Weekend mornings begin with a slow breakfast by the pool on a gently warm summer day – the perfect cappuccino from our machine and freshly picked blueberries from the nearby forest. We while away the hours by the water, swimming and reading under the parasol; as evening falls we gather on the terrace to grill with friends, watching the sun dip into the sea.'

Inside, the kitchen and dining area form the heart of the home, with daily life revolving around a generously proportioned island. Drawer fronts in oak sit against a Portland Grey limestone waterfall worktop, creating a tactile contrast.

After failing to find a dining table that matched the scale of the island, the couple commissioned a custom solid-oak table from a Danish cabinetmaker. Its top is crafted from timber reclaimed from several hundred-year-old

Natural Elements Offer Practicality

Faithful family dog Beppe patiently waits in the spacious hallway, ready for his walk. The couple selected durable limestone flooring in this area to withstand the stresses of everyday life, subtly echoing the granite rocks that lie beyond the front door and blending natural elements with practical design.

French wine presses, the weathered grain lending the piece history and soul. 'It was a significant investment,' Helena admits, 'but the clean lines, quality craftsmanship and natural materials give us confidence it will stay with us for many years.'

The couple's pursuit of quality is a consistent thread throughout the house. In the bathrooms, they commissioned custom basins carved from Norrvange limestone from Gotland – a soft, sandy-grey stone shot through with visible fossils. The material's subtle veining and fossil detail reveal something new each time you look.

Helena says the same philosophy guided their furniture and lighting choices: 'The pieces we've invested in are those we've dreamed about for years – our Spanish chairs [by Børge Mogensen] are a perfect example; we'd admired them for so long and now can't imagine parting with them.' Those chairs sit in a living-room corner beneath a four-armed Serge Mouille lamp, which turned a previously windowless nook into one of the cosiest spots in the house.

By contrast, the couple take a refreshingly pragmatic approach to soft furnishings. 'We intentionally don't spend as much on those items,' Helena explains. 'With Beppe, our dog, often claiming the sofa as his own, we didn't want to be overly precious about pieces that get heavy everyday use.'

Many of their favourite decorative finds come from Artilleriet, a beautifully-curated design shop tucked around a cobbled courtyard in central Gothenburg. Its tablescapes and vignettes offer ready-made styling inspiration, presenting furniture and objects that feel at once characterful and timeless. Visits are almost ritual: a morning spent browsing followed by coffee and a cinnamon bun at Da Matteo, a café set in a rugged old building whose rough-hewn walls and cosy seating provide the perfect counterpoint to the shop's polished displays.

Trips abroad feed the couple's imaginations further: a boutique hotel in Palma, a cafe in Paris or a shop in London. But there is one City that truly owns their hearts: Copenhagen.

'Whenever we visit, we make time to explore the city's cafés, restaurants and beautifully curated shops,' Helena explains. 'But just as inspiring are the neighbourhoods beyond the centre. We love driving along the coast just outside Copenhagen, taking in the elegant seaside villas – a mix of classic architecture and contemporary Nordic design that never fails to spark ideas.'

Back at home, the couple enjoy welcoming friends and family into the *hygge* home they have created on the hill – hosting gatherings for special occasions. To celebrate their daughter's graduation from high school, the couple set long tables on the deck dressed in white linens and pretty flowers, and laid out a buffet for more than one hundred guests, with a makeshift bar (named in honour of family dog, Beppe) created from pallets and limestone leftover from the construction.

'As we slid open our large, barn-style Crittall doors and watched the party spill effortlessly between pool, terrace and interior,' explains Helena. 'It was such a wonderful moment, to see the home we designed performing exactly as we'd hoped in this very special location.'

Framed by Nature

The dining space is enveloped on both sides by expansive Crittall windows and doors, each pane showcasing its own vignette of the rocky archipelago beyond. On clear days, diners enjoy breathtaking views stretching out to sea. On colder days, the family lights candles as rain drips down the glass, drawing the thick linen curtains for a cosy, *hygge* atmosphere.

Creating Cosy Corners

Two iconic Spanish chairs by Børge Mogensen anchor a cosy corner in the living space, set on a sleek rug from Layered Official. Jakob enjoys relaxing here – listening to music and reading – with the Serge Mouille Spider light mounted on the wall offering adjustable, focused lighting. On colder days, lighting the fire at the entrance to the kitchen adds an extra layer of warmth and comfort.

Gestures of Everyday Luxury

Many of the Scandi Modern homes we visited favoured free-standing beds without formal headboards. In Jakob and Helena's home, a relaxed feel is created by the addition of bespoke wood panelling behind the bed. On the nightstands, curated perfumes and hand creams from design-led brands like Byredo and Aesop offer indulgent moments of everyday luxury.

Scandi Modern Style Moments
that define this home

THOUGHTFUL USE OF SCALE

Big spaces can feel intimidating. Choosing furniture in the right size and scale helps to anchor such spaces. Helena and Jakob's home was one of the larger properties we visited, but felt intimate and cosy despite its generous proportions. Their large kitchen island acts as a visual anchor, grounding the open-plan layout; paired with the large, statement dining table, it somehow doesn't feel overpowering.

CURATION OF EVERY DETAIL

Curation, rather than decoration, is a cornerstone of Scandi Modern style. For example, Helena brought character and personality to her teenage sons' bedrooms, often written off as less attractive spaces, by installing open wall shelves to house treasured items: a LEGO model of a vintage Porsche, a vinyl album cover of a favourite rap artist – each piece carefully chosen to feel intentional and personal.

DESIGN FROM THE OUTSIDE IN

Designing a house from the outside helps to create a home that feels in harmony with its surroundings. Helena and Jakob's home is set into the rugged rocks that form part of the Gothenberg coastal landscape. Paying attention to this context, the couple sourced Swedish stone for their bathroom sinks and kitchen worktops, creating a shared language with the landscape through materiality.

'We wanted the house to embody functionalism and minimalism, but never at the expense of comfort.'

HELENA & JAKOB'S LIFESTYLE LIST

> **Your favourite place to holiday**

We love exploring new destinations. Norway is always high on our list for outdoor pursuits: skiing in winter or hiking in summer. Last year we visited the Lofoten Islands – undoubtedly one of the most breathtaking places we've seen. We also cherish long weekends in vibrant cities like Copenhagen and Paris; they never fail to inspire.

> **The nicest design-led accommodation you've stayed in**

The Royal Suite at SAS Radisson in Gothenburg, designed by Swedish fashion designer Lars Wallin. It's a stunning space – 160 square metres (190 square yards) of elegant glamour combined with cosy touches. When in Copenhagen, Villa Copenhagen is always a great choice.

> **On your playlist at home**

With three teenagers, the latest music is always on! Currently, 1990s hits and contemporary tunes fill our home with energy and nostalgia.

> **Your go-to design read**

The Nordic Home: Scandinavian Living, Interiors and Design. However, most of our ideas come from browsing Instagram and Pinterest, where inspiration is endless.

> **Favourite ritual for unwinding**

The moment I step into our home and catch sight of the sea, a wave of calm washes over me. I love to enjoy a freshly made cappuccino, then settle at the table, sink into the sofa or curl up in an armchair, simply gazing out over the water. It's my peaceful retreat.

> **The scent that defines your home**

I love many fragrances from Byredo, but 'Blanche' is a favourite. It perfectly defines our home – a scent that feels both clean and warm, creating an effortless sense of comfort.

THE SCANDI
JAPANESE DWELLING

When architect couple Mette Fredskild and
Masahiro Katsume began their search for a property
that could accommodate three generations of their
family (while also serving as a showroom for their
kitchen design business), it was to the Amagerbro
area of Cophenhagen that they turned.

The Amagerbro area of Copenhagen once echoed with the footsteps of factory and dock workers. The neighbourhood was carved out with purpose: simply constructed houses with brick facades lining narrow streets. Small front gardens and courtyards were designed to offer moments of respite.

Today, the neighbourhood is in a state of transformation, shedding its former identity as a working-class district and emerging as one of the city's most vibrant, multicultural enclaves – an area pulsating with new energy and diversity. 'I was drawn to the unassuming charm of the area, the authenticity in its architecture, and the honest story every building seemed to tell,' Mette explains.

After featuring Masahiro and Mette's country home in *Scandi Rustic*, we were eager to see how their unique Scandinavian-Japanese style translated to the city.

As we opened a small, brown picket-fence gate to access the house, we were struck by the way this home gradually reveals its secrets. The ground floor serves as the creative hub, where the couple work, blending craftsmanship with everyday life. Above, their daughter and her young family occupy their own floor, a tumble of toddler shoes spilling out into the hallway.

Upstairs on the second floor, white walls and pale wooden floorboards create a bright, airy space to highlight the customizable kitchens designed by Mette for the Lithuanian brand Kongacph. The designs reflect the considered simplicity that has become Mette's signature aesthetic.

The focal point of the space is a bespoke kitchen island crafted from solid oak, designed around a simple grid system. Mette explains that they 'incorporate oak off-cuts to create a design that is both durable and environmentally mindful, reducing waste.' The grid design transforms the island into a visual centrepiece, with each open shelf displaying striking ceramic pieces, including mugs made by Mette herself.

On the top floor, the same island serves as the heart of Mette's personal kitchen, seamlessly integrating with the surrounding living areas, which are tucked beneath the eaves.

Although the bones of the upstairs apartment are old, with rustic timber beams spanning the ceiling, the open-plan layout is undeniably modern. Distinct zones have been thoughtfully

Blurring Lines

The kitchen island Mette designed for Kongacph is intended to be as much a piece of furniture as a practical workspace, blurring the lines between living room and kitchen. Incorporating open shelving into the design of the island leaves room for the owner to personalize their kitchen, curating objects with personal significance to display.

'I was drawn to the unassuming charm of the area, the authenticity in its architecture, and the honest story every building seemed to tell.'

created to cater to the couple's needs. A mid-century sideboard separates a simple futon bed from the living area, flooded with natural light that streams in through a skylight above.

In their architectural practice, Mette explains: 'Our philosophy is rooted in human-centred design, creating spaces that enrich people's experiences and behaviours.' This approach makes their own home feel deeply connected to its inhabitants, supporting the rhythms of their daily lives.

A long dining table serves as a central hub, seamlessly uniting different aspects of the couple's lives. During the day, office chairs are pulled up for work, but come evening, a wooden

highchair is brought into play as their young grandson joins them for multigenerational family dinners. In the corner, sheet music rests atop a piano, while, at floor level, a miniature keyboard invites their grandson to join in the musical activities.

Unlike many Scandinavian modern homes that feature carefully curated small collections of objects, Mette and Masahiro's home exudes a sense of abundance. Yet there is intentionality to this display: shelves house collections of *Architectural Digest*, carefully gathered over the years, alongside treasured Japanese texts with weathered spines and hand-drawn characters that stand as artworks in their own right.

Modern Rustic

Mette has incorporated a bespoke island of her own design for Kongacph into her upstairs apartment. The 25 x 25mm (½ x ½ in) oak frame of the island offers a modern contrast to the thick, rustic wooden beams that otherwise define the attic space. The steel worktop adds an additional contemporary accent, creating a balanced blend of modern and historic elements.

Zoning Small Spaces

The compact upstairs apartment feels more spacious thanks to the whitewashing of the original floorboards that run throughout. Instead of walls, thoughtfully chosen pieces of furniture act as room dividers, enhancing the sense of openness: for example, the mid-century modern sideboard that separates the low futon bed in the sleeping area from the living space.

Scandi Modern Style Moments
that define this home

SMART LIVING: ZONING SPACES

Mette and Masahiro's top-floor apartment is a masterclass in how to thoughtfully zone open-plan spaces (big or small) to support daily routines and rituals. A spacious mid-century modern sideboard subtly divides the living area from the sleeping space, while a low futon bed is a visually unobstrusive choice. Office chairs doubling up as dining chairs ensure the dining table can serve two purposes.

MAXIMALIST CAN BE MINIMALIST

Compared to most of the other Scandi Modern homes we visited, Mette's apartment has more possessions. However, the displays still feel deliberate and curated; where items are abundant, such as books on floor-to-ceiling shelves, they remain within a cohesive colour palette that complements the overall design.

LET THE BUILDING'S FOUNDATIONS BE PART OF THE INTERIOR

In older homes, intentionally exposing structural elements rather than hiding them can add character and authenticity to spaces. In Mette's top-floor apartment, the exposed wooden beams crossing the ceiling add depth and warmth, celebrating the richness of the building's natural materials.

'Our architectural philosophy is rooted in human-centred design, creating spaces that enrich people's experiences and behaviours.'

MET TE'S LIFE STYLE LIST

› **Your favourite place to holiday**
Our summer retreat, about an hour from Copenhagen. It's our special haven – a place to unwind surrounded by nature's tranquility.

› **The nicest design-led accommodation you've stayed in**
Choosing a favourite is difficult. We are always drawn to places that naturally frame the landscape – minimal, no-nonsense design that integrates seamlessly with nature. This philosophy informed the black-clad cabins we designed for Konga, nestled deep in the Lithuanian forests, where simplicity and harmony reign.

› **On your playlist at home**
We have a shared love for Keith Jarrett; his contemplative jazz creates the perfect soundtrack to our daily life.

› **Your go-to design read**
Instead of books or magazines, I prefer visiting art exhibitions for inspiration. They spark my creativity and help me see spaces through a new lens.

› **Favourite ritual for unwinding**
Baking bread in the morning or enjoying a quiet, well-deserved cup of coffee after a morning run to the sea – these simple routines bring me calm.

› **The scent that defines your home**
The aroma of hinoki, a Japanese cedar, defines our home. Its calming, woody scent brings a sense of freshness and connection to nature that we cherish deeply.

THE COSY &
COCOONING
APARTMENT

Just across the bridge from Christianshavn,
one of Copenhagen's most historic and bohemian
neighbourhoods, Oliver and Michelle have created a calm,
inviting home within an apartment that once served as
a shop in a previous era of the building's history.

Styling Storage

A large shelving system in the dining room opens up opportunities for styling. Oliver enjoys creating vignettes with art, books and personal items. Many of the pieces are from Danish artists or brands, with an emphasis on organic shapes and natural materials.

Oliver and Michelle, along with their baby daughter and their faithful dog Marcelo, are beginning to put down roots after completing three renovations in just three years to move up the property ladder in Copenhagen, a city whose housing market rivals London and New York in pricing.

Michelle explains that while their renovation projects began as a necessity, driven by a limited budget, the process has since transformed into a passion, for Oliver in particular. His sharp eye for interiors and meticulous attention to detail have helped craft a Scandi Modern style that is beautifully pared back and minimalist, yet never feels cold or sterile. Instead, the apartment exudes warmth and serenity.

Michelle laughs that she never knows what to expect when she wakes up. 'Inspiration often strikes Oliver at night – to experiment with new furniture layouts or ways to display our objects,' she says. 'For me, it's like a game to guess what has moved overnight – it's always a pleasant surprise, though.'

At the heart of the home is a dining space, where the young family gather for leisurely breakfasts at a circular table crafted from travertine by iconic Danish brand GUBI. To soften the stone of the table, woven chairs have been paired with it, and the couple's baby daughter's highchair is an equally stylish seat at the table, in soft neutral tones and wood.

At weekends, Oliver often walks Marcelo to fetch pastries from Bodenhoffs bakery, one of Copenhagen's oldest and most celebrated bakeries. On our visit we sampled a selection of golden flaky treats, including a Spandauer, a custard-filled pastry almost as irresistible as the city's beloved cinnamon buns.

Though the apartment fronts a busy street, soft linen and gauze curtains cocoon the living space, filtering out the city beyond. The room is thoughtfully curated – coffee and sidetables are arranged with beloved ceramics and books – but it also functions as a practical family hub, with clever, discreet storage so that everyday life doesn't disturb the carefully curated aesthetic. The sofa converts into a bed, with cushions and winter blankets neatly stashed in an underseat compartment, while jute baskets tucked into corners hide the baby's toys until playtime.

When we asked the couple which aspect of the renovation they are most pleased with, they answered without hesitation: the kitchen. Created by knocking down and expanding a room previously used as a child's bedroom, it is here that Olivier's attention to detail really shines. He explains: 'The oak cabinets were built by a friend in the joinery business, to my specification.' The stainless-steel worktops the couple have selected could feel utilitarian in another setting, but lighting has been cleverly layered together to bath the room in a warm glow that softens the metal. A distinctive linen pendant light from Audo Copenhagen runs the length of the island, creating a focal point, while recessed spotlights pool light over the worktops. A single open shelf above the worktops is carefully curated, with negative space allowing the objects on display breath.

The couple's bedroom leads off the kitchen with a soft neutral colour palette creating a cocooning atmosphere. Visual distraction is minimized by the addition of inbuilt wardrobes. Oliver explains that these are 'simple IKEA carcasses and then the fronts were painted in the same neutral shades as the walls:' a cost-effective solution that creates a quietly luxurious feel to the space. Contemporary oak panelling that echos the style and tone of the kitchen cabinets has been added behind the bed, subtly tying the two spaces together.

Oliver's intentional approach to the design of the room extends even to functional items such as the radiator covers, which were made bespoke to match the materiality of the rest of the room.

The family bathroom is small in footprint but feels much more expansive as a result of the choice to add a full-wall mirror to one wall. Bathroom sinks can often become cluttered spaces; the decison to recess the travertine sink within a bespoke vanity cabinet minimizes this risk. Soft fluffy towels from Danish brand Tekal, in a rich chocolatey brown, provide a tactile contrast to the harder surfaces.

In common with many apartment buildings in Copenhagen, at the rear their home opens onto a communal courtyard, which Michelle explains: 'From early afternoon this slowly comes to life as children return from daycare and school.'

Perhaps more unusually for this neighbourhood (and a key factor in their decision to purchase the apartment), the couple also enjoy use of an outdoor space that wraps around the front of their home. It still has a slightly wild quality to it at the moment, with views of the golden spiralled turret of the Church of Our Saviour glimmering through a tangle of trees. However, Oliver has plans for its transformation. He shared with us that he 'would like to add custom decking and a proper area for outdoor dining, and perhaps storage for our bikes, to conceal them a little more from view.'

In-frame Design

The kitchen features a deep in-frame system with no visible handles, complemented by recessed grips integrated into the frame, for a sleek, seamless appearance. Tall cabinets are push-to-open, maintaining uniformity across the design. Constructing all cabinets, drawers and units from a single piece of wood allows the grain to flow uninterrupted from top to bottom, enhancing the cabinetry's visual harmony.

Shelf Styling

In the kitchen, a single open shelf runs along the wall, cut from the same piece of wood as the kitchen units and therefore preserving simplicity, while allowing for storytelling through curated objects. Ceramic bowls are displayed alongside warm wood accents, with metallic egg cups subtly echoing the worktop's finish. The built-in shelving above the coffee machine demonstrates how even a functional space can serve as an opportunity for stylish expression.

Family-friendly Design

The couple's living room combines style and functionality. At its heart is a sofa bed from Danish brand Frama that perfects the dual purpose of hosting impromptu movie nights while providing discreet storage for blankets, cushions and pillows. The design of the room reflects the couple's philosophy that their home should be aesthetically pleasing without compromising the reality of day-to-day family life.

Cocooning Spaces

A cocooning atmosphere is achieved in the bedroom through layered linen and gauze curtains, complemented by soft linen bedding in neutral tones. A delicate paper pendant suspended above the bed adds visual interest without overpowering the space, enhancing the room's tranquil feeling.

Reflect to Amplify

In the compact apartment bathroom, clever design amplifies the sense of space. A full-wall mirror has been added above the basin, while a travertine sink, seamlessly set into a bespoke vanity, combines practicality with refined craftsmanship. The couple are Aesop lovers and the company's signature sensory blends diffuse into the air.

Beside the Bed

Matching bedside tables handmade in Denmark are in the same wood finish as the bespoke panelling behind the bed, seamlessly integrating the two elements; these tables also offer discreet storage. Lamps on either side of the bed from Vitra's Ankari series cast soft ambient light, further enhancing the cosy atmosphere of the room.

Scandi Modern Style Moments
that define this home

INVESTING IN DESIGN CLASSICS

Affordable homeware brands make an interior feel contemporary; investment in Swedish and Danish heritage brands make it feel timeless. Oliver and Michelle mix the two together effortlessly. For example, they patiently waited for the GUBI sample sale to acquire their circular travertine table, which adds a sense of soft luxury to their dining space.

ADDING BESPOKE DETAILS

Bespoke joinery solutions are used to craft a seamless interior with a flowing aesthetic. This personalized approach doesn't have to be costly; a luxurious feel can be achieved by using IKEA Pax wardrobes with custom-made doors, or thoughtfully (and sparingly) incorporating high-quality materials. Oliver, for instance, enhanced their bedroom with slimline oak panelling behind the bed, adding a sophisticated and tailored finish.

SEASONAL STYLING CHANGE

Scandi Modern style attentively responds to the changing seasons. In this home, we loved the unique wall-hung set of bookshelves from Mistral Furniture, housing books and ceramics with displays thoughtfully updated through the seasons. The small vases hold single blooms of fresh flowers in summer, but arrangements become more subdued as the seasons change, featuring dried grasses in muted colours.

'Inspiration often strikes Oliver at night – to experiment with new furniture layouts or ways to display our objects …It's like a game to guess what has moved overnight.'

OLIVER & MICHELLE'S LIFESTYLE LIST

❯ Your favourite place to holiday

Mexico was a trip we both loved, filled with lasting memories, and Spain (Málaga in particular) will always hold a special place in our hearts; it's where we first met and we share a deep connection to its vibrant culture.

❯ The nicest design-led accommodation you've stayed in

We dream of visiting Bali, to create more unforgettable moments as a family and soak up the extraordinary design scene there. Capella Ubud, an architect-designed tent retreat, is on our bucket list of places to stay.

❯ On your playlist at home

Our playlist varies according to the season and mood. Bon Iver – an artist Oliver grew up with – is a favourite; the calming soundscape always brings peace. We love blending different genres to suit our atmosphere.

❯ Your go-to design read

The Danish magazine *RUM* is a constant source of inspiration, with its fresh perspectives on modern Scandinavian design. We also enjoy the beautifully curated projects of Norm Architects, which challenge and inspire our creative thinking.

❯ Favourite ritual for unwinding

Quiet evenings at home, spending quality time together. Rainy days in Denmark are often spent with candles lit, aromatic oils diffusing and plenty of blankets and pillows. When we want to fully relax, we order in dinner, turn the sofa into a bed layered with duvets and watch a film together.

❯ The scent that defines your home

We are avid fans of Aesop, and 'Marrakech Intense' has become part of our signature atmosphere – its warm, spicy notes often fill the air in our apartment.

Source List

LIVING ROOM

Att Pynta
attpynta.com

Audo Copenhagen
audocph.com

Bolia
bolia.com

Broste Copenhagen
brostecopenhagen.com

Castlery
castlery.com

Cooee Design
cooee.eu

Ferm Living
fermliving.com

Fredericia
fredericia.com

Gallery At Home
galleryathome.co.uk

Georg Jensen
georgjensen.com

GUBI
gubi.com

Heathfield & Co
heathfield.co.uk

King Maker Studio
kingmaker-studio.com

Loewe
loewe.com

Muuto
muuto.com

My Theresa Life
mytheresa.com

Nest
nest.co.uk

Nkuku
nkuku.com

Nordic Knots
nordicknots.com

Pooky
pooky.com

Rajan Seth
artbyrajanseth.com

Restoration Hardware
rh.com

Six the Residence
sixtheresidence.com

Skandinavisk
skandinavisk.com

Soho Home
sohohome.com

Spark & Bell
sparkandbell.com

Target
target.com

Tine K Home
tinekhome.com

Vinterior
vinterior.co

West Elm
westelm.com

Zara Home
zarahome.com

DINING ROOM

&Tradition
andtradition.com

Another Country
anothercountry.com

Atelliert
artilleriet.se

Baileys Home Store
baileyshome.com

Carl Hansen & Søn
carlhansen.com

Crate & Barrel
crateandbarrel.com

Fritz Hansen
fritzhansen.com

Glassette
glassette.com

Hay
hay.com

Lagom Glassware
lagomglassware.com

Mater
materdesign.com

Neptune
neptune.com

NUDE Glass
nudeglass.com

Rowen & Wren
rowenandwren.co.uk

Stoff Nagel
stoffnagel.com

Wabi Sabi Nordic
wabisabinordic.com

KITCHEN

Ask og Eng
askogeng.no

Borough Kitchen
boroughkitchen.com

Caesarstone
caesarstone.co.uk

Corston Architectural
corston.com

Cosentino
cosentino.com

Daylesford
daylesford.com

deVOL
devolkitchens.co.uk

Dor & Tan
dorandtan.com

EOT Ceramics
eotceramics.com

Grain & Knot
grainandknot.com

Ikea
ikea.com

John Lewis
johnlewis.com

The Main Company
maincompany.co.uk

Normann Copenhagen
normann-copenhagen.com

Nordiska Kök
nordiskakok.com

Reform
reformcph.com

Sola Kitchens
solakitchens.com

String Furniture
stringfurniture.com

Vipp
vipp.com

Williams Sonoma
williams-sonoma.com

BEDROOM

Anthropologie
anthropologie.com

Bed Threads
bedthreads.co.uk

Bedfolk
bedfolk.com

By Nord
bynord.nl

Heals
heals.com

Naturalmat
naturalmat.co.uk

Nordic Nest
nordicnest.com

Paper Collective
papercollective.com

Pottery Barn
potterybarn.co.uk

Rise & Fall
riseandfall.co

Tekla
teklafabrics.com

Waxed Floors
waxedfloors.co.uk

The White Company
thewhitecompany.com

BATHROOM

Aesop
aesop.com

Bert & May
bertandmay.com

Bespoke Taps
bespoketaps.com

Detale Copenhagen
detalecph.com

Duravit
duravit.com

Festfloor
festfloor.com

Frama
framacph.com

H&M Home
hm.com

Lusso Stone
lussostone.com

Malin & Goetz
malinandgoetz.com

Mandarin Stone
mandarinstone.com

Otto Tiles
ottotiles.com

Silent Gliss
silentgliss.com

Verden
verden.world

Vola
vola.com

GARDEN & OUTDOOR

And Four Studio
andfour.com

Cane-line
cane-line.com

Dig
digclub.co.uk

Homebarn
homebarnshop.co.uk

Nth Degree
nthdegree.co.uk

Homeowners

REENA + MATT
PAGES 70–87

Reena, a creative director, author, designer and founder of Hygge for Home, lives in a modern, Scandinavian-inspired black-clad house in Wales, together with her husband Matt, a software engineer, and their three daughters. Together they've created a home where light, texture and natural materials offer a sense of calm in the chaos of family life. Warm, modern and intentionally designed, it's a space shaped around connection and everyday rituals that encourages slowing down and invites cosiness. Reena is the co-author with Rebecca of *Scandi Rustic*.

REBECCA + GARETH
PAGES 88–105

Rebecca, a sustainability professional and founder of Malmo & Moss, lives in North London together with her lawyer husband Gareth and their three sons. After outgrowing their first home, an Edwardian terrace, they were drawn to the wider footprint and quiet potential of their current 1930s house. Their 18-month renovation project created a light-filled, open space shaped by Scandinavian simplicity and natural materials. For Rebecca, the home is a grounding sanctuary, a place where family life can unfold with ease, supported by thoughtful design and a calm, cohesive palette.

ELLE + ROBIN
PAGES 106–17

Elle lives in East London with her Swedish husband Robin, her stepson and their golden retriever, Max. As the Design Director of Ett Hem London (EHL STUDIO), she combines creative direction with interior styling. With a photographer father and ceramicist mother, a strong interest in creative pursuits has always been in her DNA. The Victorian townhouse Elle and her family call home reflects a unique Scandinavian-British sensibility.

NAMALI + LINUS
PAGES 118–35

Namali lives on the Spanish island of Mallorca with her two teenage children and partner Linus (a former Tour de France cyclist). Born in Sri Lanka and raised in Germany, her love of gathering and storytelling led her from a career in TV production to founding the restaurant Nama in Deià. The couple run Soul Escapes, a property development business, creating unique homes on the island. Namali also works as an interior designer, shaping homes across the world with warmth, texture and soul. Her own house reflects her instinctive eye, a Scandi-modern sanctuary layered with heritage, craft and intention.

KINE + KRISTOFFER
PAGES 136–51

Native Norwegians, Kine and Kristoffer live and work in the village of Binssalem on Mallorca with their two young sons. Kine has a background in environmental geography, while Kristoffer is an architect. Together they co-founded Ask og Eng, an interior design practice that blends sustainability, material honesty and thoughtful simplicity. Their Mallorcan townhouse serves as both home and creative studio – a warm, conscious, evolving space that reflects their shared values and love of nature.

SOFIA + JON
PAGES 152–65

Sofia and Jon live on the East Coast of Sweden, near Kalmar, with their two young sons. They returned to the area after years spent living in Stockholm to be closer to family. Sofia is Head of Social Media and Affiliate Marketing at Nordic Nest Group, while Jon works as Head of Communications and Marketing at Destination Kalmar. Their home sits on a historic plot, carved from the garden of a neighbour, framed by oak trees and the sea. Designed with light, openness and gathering in mind, it's a warm, modern space with a deep connection to the landscape.

HELENA + JAKOB

PAGES 166–83

Helena and Jakob, a business consultant, live in a distinctive black-clad family home near Gothenberg, with their three teenage children and Labrador, Beppe. After many years spent working in finance and fashion, overseeing the design and build of their home has led to a new career for Helena in interior design and content creation. Together the couple have created a modern *hygge*-feeling space, uniquely informed by the rocky archipelago in which it is nestled.

METTE + MATSUTO

PAGES 184–197

Architects Mette and Matsuto live in Amagerbro, Copenhagen, in a three-generation home that also serves as a creative base for their shared design practice. Known for their distinctive Scandinavian–Japanese aesthetic, they create human-centred spaces shaped by calm simplicity, craftsmanship and natural materials. Their home reflects this philosophy: light-filled rooms, bespoke oak joinery and curated ceramics that carry personal meaning. Designed for working and gathering, it's a space that evolves with the family while honouring the quiet authenticity of the neighbourhood around it.

OLIVER + MICHELLE

PAGES 198–215

Oliver and Michelle live in central Copenhagen with their daughter Ella and dog Marcello. After moving to the city for fresh career opportunities, they discovered a shared passion for transforming old apartments: completing three full renovations in just a few years. Michelle works as Head of Internal Media, while Oliver works in commercial partnerships, both channelling their creativity into designing calm, functional Japandi-inspired spaces. Their current 1915 apartment is their most personal project yet – a cosy apartment shaped by thoughtful materials, clever craftsmanship, and the balance of city life and nature on their doorstep.

Acknowledgements

BENJAMIN EDWARDS

To our brilliant friend and photographer, thank you for seeing our vision before it fully existed. You didn't just capture homes, you captured the warmth, the texture, the life within them. Your eye shaped this book as much as our words did, and your patience, humour and generosity carried us through long shoots, early mornings and endless cups of tea. We are forever grateful for the way you helped us bring this world to life.

OCTOPUS TEAM

To the extraordinary team at Octopus, thank you Alison and Jonathan especially for guiding this book with such care. Your belief in our perspective, your trust in our voice and your editorial clarity helped us refine every page. We are endlessly thankful for your steady support, your creative freedom and your commitment to making this book the best version of itself.

OUR FAMILIES

To our husbands Gareth and Matt, who held the fort with six children and juggled dinners, school runs, laundry mountains and bedtime stories so we could travel, write and shoot across three countries. We could not have done this without you. And to our six children, you are our biggest inspiration, and the reason for everything that we do.

HOMEOWNERS

To the generous homeowners who welcomed us into your beautiful homes, thank you for trusting us with your stories, your rituals and every corner of your spaces. The commitment and care in your creative choices shaped the narrative of this book. We are so honoured you let us step into your worlds and will be forever grateful that you came on this journey with us. This book is much yours as it is ours.

OUR COMMUNITY

Thank you for walking beside us for so many years, and for waiting six whole years for us to put pen to paper and write another book. You are the reason we dared to believe that a love of Scandi design, cosy living and intentional homes could become something bigger. Your messages, your encouragement, your curiosity and your constant presence gave us the courage to write this book. You allowed us to live out our Scandi dreams, and we carry you with us on every page.

Index